NORWAY TRAVEL GUIDE 2025

Explore Fjords, Northern Lights, and Must-See Destinations with Expert Tips, Road Trip Hacks, Detailed Maps, and Stunning Images for an Unforgettable Scandinavian Adventure

Albert S. Swim

Disclaimer

Welcome to **Norway Travel Guide for 2025!** Get ready to fall in love with one of the world's most stunning countries. From majestic fjords to snow-capped peaks, vibrant cities to charming coastal villages, Norway has it all.

This guide is packed with local tips and insider secrets. Whether you're chasing the Northern Lights, cruising along the fjords, or exploring scenic hiking trails, we've got you covered.

Quick tip: Norway's weather can change quickly, so be prepared and plan accordingly for every adventure.

Think of me as your Norway friend, here to help you discover both famous sights and hidden gems. Your 2025 journey will be unforgettable!

Happy exploring!

TABLE OF CONTENTS

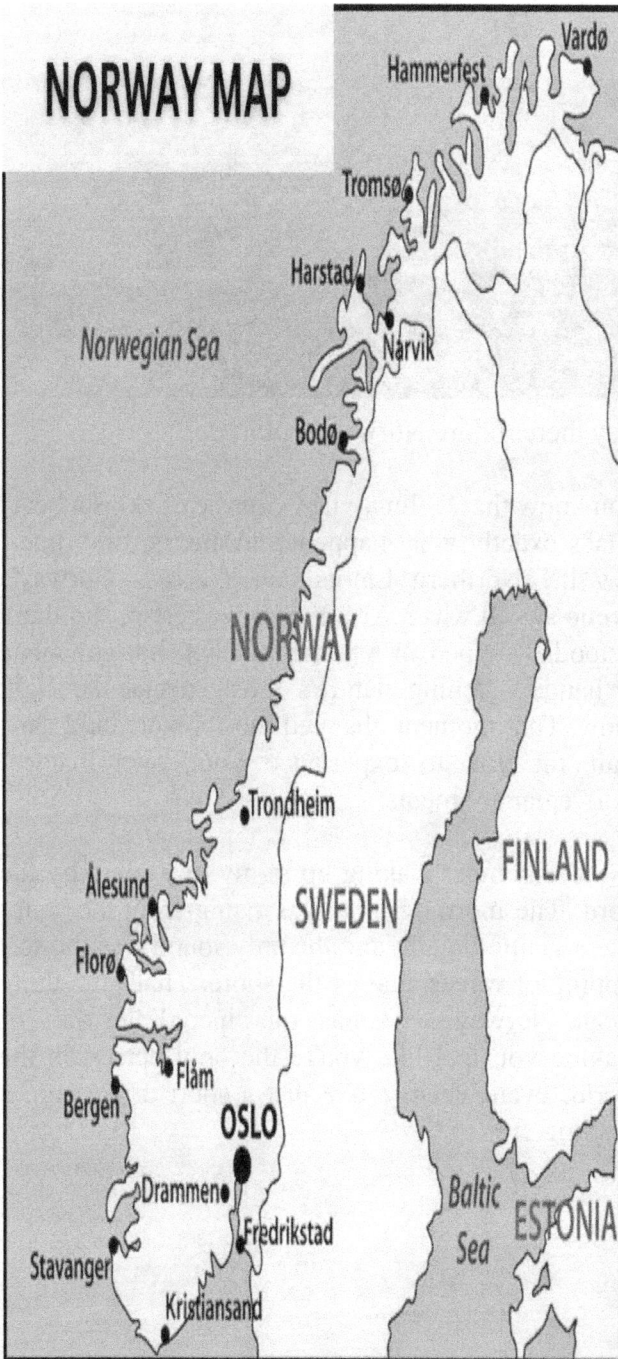

NORWAY MAP

INTRODUCTION

Hey there, future Norway explorer!

You know that feeling when your heart skips a beat? That's exactly what happened to me the first time I saw the Northern Lights dance across Norway's Arctic sky. It was 3 AM, the air was crisp, and there I stood, wrapped in a warm blanket, hot chocolate in hand, watching nature's most spectacular light show. That moment changed me forever, and I can't wait for you to experience your own magical Norwegian moments.

I still remember waking up in my tiny cabin by the fjord. The morning mist was rising from the water like a gentle breath, and the only sound was the soft lapping of waves against the shore. That's the thing about Norway – it has this incredible way of making you feel like you're the only person in the world, even when you're just a short drive from a bustling city.

Let me share another secret: there's nothing quite like biting into a warm skillingsboller (Norwegian cinnamon bun) on a chilly Bergen morning. I found this little bakery tucked away between the colorful wooden houses of Bryggen – the kind of place where grandmothers still bake using recipes passed down through generations. The owner, Mari, now greets me like family whenever I visit, and yes, I'll tell you exactly where to find her!

But it's not just the places – it's the people. Norwegians have this wonderful way of making you feel at home. Like Thor, the fisherman who invited me to join his family's midsummer celebration in the Lofoten Islands. We grilled fresh-caught fish under the midnight sun, shared stories, and laughed until the sky turned pink (which, in summer, might mean 2 AM!).

This guide isn't just a collection of places to see – it's my love letter to Norway. Every recommendation comes from real experiences, every secret spot has a story, and every tip is written with the hope that you'll fall in love with this incredible country just like I did.

Ready to begin your Norwegian adventure? Let's explore together – from thundering waterfalls to cozy cafés, from Arctic adventures to peaceful fjord moments. Your own Norwegian story is waiting to unfold.

Velkommen to Norway 2025!

Chapter 1: Discovering Norway at a Glance

A. A Brief History of Norway

Hello!

Before you pack your bags for this epic Scandinavian escape, let's take a quick stroll through Norway's past. Trust me, the history here is as majestic as the fjords you'll be marveling at soon.

Imagine this: Thousands of years ago, Norway was a frozen wilderness inhabited by people who hunted, fished, and gathered food to survive. Over time, small communities formed, and by the Viking Age (around 800-1050 AD), Norway had become home to some of the most fearless explorers the world has ever known. These seafaring warriors weren't just about raiding and conquering—they were also skilled traders and storytellers, spreading Norse culture across Europe and beyond.

Fast forward a bit, and you'll find Norway transforming into a kingdom under King Harald Fairhair, who united the country in the 9th century. During the medieval period, Christianity swept through Norway, leaving behind those stunning stave churches you'll definitely want to see. But Norway wasn't always independent. For centuries, it was part of unions with Denmark and Sweden, which shaped its culture and politics in big ways.

Then came 1905, a year that changed everything. Norway peacefully broke away from Sweden and became the independent nation we know today. And here's a fun twist: just a few decades later, Norway struck black gold—oil—in the North Sea. This discovery turned the country into one of the wealthiest in the world, but instead of splurging, Norway became a global leader in sustainability and green energy.

What's even cooler? While Norway is all about modern innovation, its deep connection to nature and tradition remains untouched. The people here value the simple joys—like hiking in the mountains, foraging in the woods, and gathering around a cozy fire to share stories.

So, what does all this history mean for your trip? It means every fjord, museum, and historic site you visit has a story to tell. Norway isn't just a place to see; it's a place to experience, where the past and present come together in ways you won't find anywhere else.

Get ready to explore a land of Vikings, breathtaking landscapes (oops, scratch that—jaw-dropping views!), and a culture that's as warm as a freshly baked Kanelboller. Your Norwegian adventure is about to begin, and it's going to be incredible!

B. Why Visit and What's New in Norway for 2025?

Thinking about adding Norway to your travel bucket list? Let me give you the lowdown on why 2025 is the perfect time to experience this Scandinavian gem. From its awe-inspiring landscapes to cutting-edge attractions, Norway is gearing up to offer travelers an unforgettable adventure.

Nature's Playground

Imagine this: towering fjords, cascading waterfalls, and the mesmerizing dance of the Northern Lights.

Norway's natural beauty is nothing short of spectacular. Whether you're hiking through lush forests, cruising along serene fjords, or chasing the aurora borealis, every moment here feels like stepping into a postcard.

What's New in 2025?

Norway is not just resting on its natural laurels; 2025 brings a slew of exciting developments:

- **Norient Express:** Starting in autumn 2025, embark on a six-day luxury train journey aboard the Norient Express. This eco-friendly train will whisk you from the coastal city of Bergen, through Oslo, to the historic city of Trondheim, offering panoramic views of Norway's breathtaking landscapes.

- **SKREI Experience Center:** Set to open in 2026 in Lofoten, SKREI will be a hub for all things related to the iconic Norwegian cod. The center will feature interactive exhibits, virtual reality experiences, and insights into the fishing heritage that has shaped Norway.

- **Cultural Renaissance in Bodø:** Named the European Capital of Culture for 2024, Bodø is continuing its cultural transformation into 2025. With new art galleries, music festivals, and cultural events, the city offers a vibrant arts scene set against the backdrop of stunning natural beauty.

Sustainable Tourism

Norway is leading the charge in sustainable travel. By summer 2025, the country plans to implement a tourist tax aimed at preserving its pristine environments and supporting local communities. This initiative ensures that your visit contributes positively to the places you explore.

Culinary Delights

Foodies, rejoice! Norway's culinary scene is blossoming with farm-to-table experiences and a focus on local, organic ingredients. In September 2024, the Michelin-starred restaurant Credo relocated to Oslo, offering a new dining and cultural concept in collaboration with the National Library of Norway. This trend of innovative dining is set to continue into 2025, providing gastronomic adventures that tantalize the taste buds.

Adventure Awaits

From the thrill of dog sledding in Tromsø to the serenity of kayaking through the fjords, Norway offers a plethora of activities for every type of traveler. In 2025, new hiking trails and adventure parks are set to open, providing even more opportunities to immerse yourself in the great outdoors.

C. How to Use This Guide Effectively

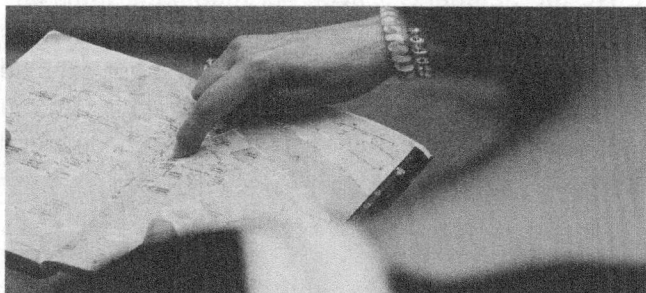

Let me show you how to use it effectively so you can dive straight into the fjords, cities, and beyond without missing a beat.

Start with the Basics
If you're new to Norway, the first chapters are your go-to. They'll give you a quick history lesson and the must-know facts about the country. This isn't just trivia—it'll help you understand why Norway's culture, landscapes, and lifestyle are so unique. Knowing a little backstory will make your trip feel that much richer.

Plan Like a Pro
This guide is organized to help you tackle Norway one step at a time. Not sure where to begin? Head to the chapters on must-see destinations and top activities. Whether you're drawn to the buzzing energy of Oslo, the quiet charm of Bergen, or the wild beauty of the Arctic Circle, this guide breaks it all down for you.

Customize Your Journey
Every traveler is different, and this guide gets that. Love the outdoors? Check out the hiking trails and fjord adventures. Big on food? Flip to the sections on local dishes and dining tips. We've got detailed itineraries for short trips and longer stays, so you can tailor your experience to fit your schedule and interests.

Use the Insider Tips
Sprinkled throughout this book are insider tips—little nuggets of wisdom from locals and experienced travelers. These are the kind of things you won't find in a quick Google search, like the best times to visit popular spots or hidden gems off the beaten path. Keep an eye out for these—they're pure gold!

Stay Practical
Traveling can be unpredictable, but this guide has you covered. From navigating Norway's excellent public transportation system to understanding local customs, the practical advice in here will save you time, money, and stress. There's even a section on eco-friendly travel tips to help you explore responsibly.

Keep It Handy
This isn't a book you read once and forget—it's your travel buddy. Take it with you on the plane, keep it nearby while packing, and flip through it

during your downtime. Use it to plan your days or find quick answers when you're out and about.

Chapter 2: Planning Your Norwegian Trip

A. Getting to Norway: Best Flights to Consider

Flying is one of the fastest and most convenient ways to reach Norway, a land of majestic fjords and Arctic wonders. To help you plan your journey, here's an updated guide to the best airports and flights for your Norwegian adventure.

1. Oslo Gardermoen Airport (OSL)

Oslo Gardermoen Airport

Oslo Airport
Edvard Munchs veg, 2061
Gardermoen, Norway

4.3 ★★★★★

View larger map

Directions

Lufthavn

Google

Keyboard shortcuts   Map data ©2024   Terms

SCAN THE QR CODE

1. Open your device camera app.

2. Position the QR code in the camera frame.

3. Hold your phone steady.

4. Wait for the code to be recognized.

5. Once recognized, tap on the notification or follow the prompt to access the content or action associated with the Qr code

- **Location**: Just 22 miles (35 km) northeast of Oslo's city center.
- **Why It's Awesome:** As Norway's busiest international hub, Oslo Gardermoen offers smooth connections from cities like New York, London, and Tokyo. The airport boasts modern facilities, fantastic lounges, and seamless train services to Oslo in under 20 minutes (210 NOK or ~$20).
- **Airlines:** Major carriers like SAS, Norwegian Air Shuttle, Lufthansa, and Delta operate here, offering year-round flights.
- **Cost:** Round-trip flights range from $600 to $1,200 from New York, and $100 to $300 from London.
- **Website & Contact:** [Oslo Airport](https://avinor.no/en/airport/oslo-airport), +47 64 81 20 00.

2. Bergen Airport, Flesland (BGO)

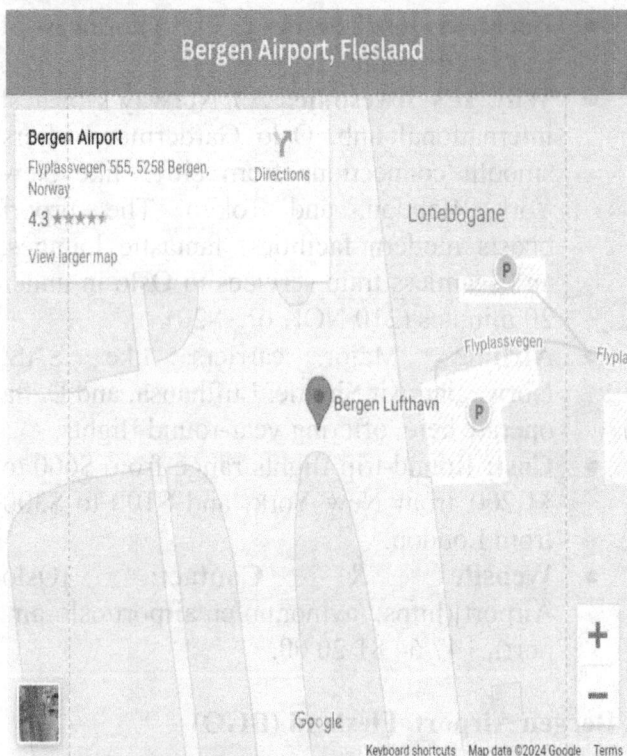

Bergen Airport, Flesland

Bergen Airport
Flyplassvegen 555, 5258 Bergen, Norway
4.3 ★★★★★
View larger map

Directions

Lonebogane

Bergen Lufthavn

SCAN THE QR CODE

1. Open your device camera app.
2. Position the QR code in the camera frame.
3. Hold your phone steady.
4. Wait for the code to be recognized.
5. Once recognized, tap on the notification or follow the prompt to access the content or action associated with the Qr code

- **Location**: About 12 miles (20 km) southwest of Bergen.
- **Why It's Awesome:** Bergen Airport is perfect if you're headed to Norway's western fjords. It's smaller than Oslo but just as efficient, with easy Light Rail connections to Bergen city (45 minutes, 40 NOK or ~$4).
- **Airlines:** SAS, KLM, and Norwegian Air Shuttle operate frequent flights here.
- **Cost:** Round-trips range from $120 to $250 from London and $150 to $300 from Amsterdam.
- **Website & Contact:** [Bergen Airport](https://avinor.no/en/airport/bergen-airport), +47 67 03 11 00.

3. Stavanger Airport, Sola (SVG)

Stavanger Airport, Sola

Stavanger Airport

Flyplassvegen 230, 4055 Sola, Norway

4.3 ★★★★★

View larger map

Directions

Stavanger lufthavn Sola

Google

Keyboard shortcuts Map data ©2024 Google Terms

SCAN THE QR CODE

1. Open your device camera app.
2. Position the QR code in the camera frame.
3. Hold your phone steady.
4. Wait for the code to be recognized.
5. Once recognized, tap on the notification or follow the prompt to access the content or action associated with the Qr code

- **Location**: 7 miles (11 km) southwest of Stavanger.
- **Why It's Awesome:** Ideal for accessing Preikestolen (Pulpit Rock), Stavanger Airport is a cozy and efficient hub. It offers smooth taxi (450 NOK or ~$42) and bus transfers to the city center.
- **Airlines:** SAS, Norwegian, and Lufthansa offer flights here.
- **Cost:** Flights range from $120 to $250 from London and $90 to $200 from Copenhagen.
- **Website & Contact:** [Stavanger Airport](https://avinor.no/en/airport/stavanger-airport), +47 67 03 10 00.

4. Tromsø Airport, Langnes (TOS)

Tromsø Airport, Langnes

Tromsø Airport
Flyplassvegen 31, 9016 Tromsø, Norway
3.6 ★★★☆☆
View larger map

Directions

Tromsø lufthavn

Google

Keyboard shortcuts   Map data ©2024 Google   Terms

SCAN THE QR CODE

1. Open your device camera app.
2. Position the QR code in the camera frame.
3. Hold your phone steady.
4. Wait for the code to be recognized.
5. Once recognized, tap on the notification or follow the prompt to access the content or action associated with the Qr code

- **Location**: Just 3 miles (5 km) from Tromsø's city center.
- **Why It's Awesome:** Known for Northern Lights and Arctic adventures, Tromsø Airport is a must for winter travelers. Affordable buses connect the airport to the city (100 NOK or ~$9).
- **Airlines:** SAS, Norwegian, and Widerøe serve this scenic gateway.
- **Cost:** Round-trips range from $120 to $300 from Oslo and $250 to $450 from London.
- **Website & Contact:** [Tromsø Airport](https://avinor.no/en/airport/tromso-airport), +47 67 03 10 00.

Booking Tips:
- **Book Early:** Flights to Norway are cheaper when reserved months ahead.
- **Travel Off-Season:** Spring and autumn offer lower fares than the busy summer or winter seasons.
- **Use Travel Apps:** Tools like Skyscanner can help find deals across airlines.

B. Public Transportation

Getting around Norway is not only efficient but also a part of the adventure. To make your travel stress-free, here's everything you need to know about navigating Norway's world-class transport system.

1. Trains

- **Location & Coverage:** Norway's train network, operated by Vy, connects major cities like Oslo, Bergen, Stavanger, and Trondheim, and even stretches into rural towns.
- **Why It's Awesome:** The Bergen Line, connecting Oslo and Bergen, is often called one of the most beautiful train journeys in the world, with its dramatic mountain views and endless fjords. Trains are comfortable, eco-friendly, and reliable.
- **Cost:** Prices for long-distance routes like Oslo to Bergen start at 249 NOK (~$23) when booked early.
- **Good to Know:** Trains are equipped with free Wi-Fi, power outlets, and snacks for purchase. Booking early on [Vy's Website](https://www.vy.no) ensures you get the best fares.

2. Buses

- **Location & Coverage:** Norway's buses fill in the gaps where trains can't reach, making them ideal for exploring smaller towns and off-the-beaten-path destinations. Companies like NOR-WAY Bussekspress and Vy Buss operate across the country.
- **Why It's Awesome:** Buses are affordable and flexible, with routes covering everything from urban centers to remote villages. In

cities like Oslo and Bergen, local buses are integrated into the public transport system for seamless travel.

- **Cost:** Local city rides start at 35 NOK (~$3), while intercity journeys like Oslo to Kristiansand cost around 300 NOK (~$28).
- **Good to Know:** Tickets can be purchased through apps like Ruter (Oslo) or directly from the driver. Local buses often operate on a cashless system, so a travel card or app is handy.

3. Trams

- **Location & Coverage:** Available in cities like Oslo and Trondheim, trams are perfect for exploring urban centers while taking in the sights.
- **Why It's Awesome**: Trams stop near major attractions, like Oslo's Royal Palace and Vigeland Sculpture Park, offering both convenience and charm.
- **Cost**: A single ride costs about 35 NOK (~$3), with unlimited travel passes for 24 hours starting at 105 NOK (~$10).
- **Good to Know**: Tickets must be validated before boarding to avoid fines. Apps like Ruter are a lifesaver for planning and purchasing tram journeys.

4. Ferries

- **Location & Coverage:** Norway's ferries connect coastal towns, islands, and fjords. Services like Hurtigruten also offer multi-day cruises with spectacular views of Norway's coastline.
- **Why It's Awesome:** Ferries are more than transport—they're part of the experience. Routes like the Geirangerfjord ferry let you witness UNESCO-listed landscapes up close.
- **Cost:** Prices vary by route, but a short ferry ride costs around 50 NOK (~$5). Longer fjord cruises start at 500 NOK (~$47).
- **Good to Know:** Many ferries accommodate cars, making them perfect for road trips. Tickets can be booked on-site or through the ferry company's website.

5. Travel Apps

Apps like Entur and Ruter are invaluable. They provide real-time schedules, ticket options, and route planning for all modes of transport across Norway. These user-friendly tools will help you navigate like a local.

Pro Tips for Public Transport in Norway

- **Eco-Friendly Travel:** Many buses and ferries run on electricity or hybrid systems, so you're exploring sustainably.

- **Timetables:** Services in rural areas might be limited, so plan your journeys ahead of time, especially during weekends and holidays.
- **Payment:** Most public transport is cashless, so be ready with a credit card, mobile payment app, or travel card.

Chapter 3: Practical Information

A. Visa and Entry Requirements

Before you pack your bags for the land of fjords and northern lights, let's get you up to speed on the latest visa and entry requirements for 2025. Staying informed ensures a smooth journey, so here's what you need to know:

Schengen Visa Overview

Norway is part of the Schengen Area, which allows for passport-free travel among member countries. Depending on your nationality, you may need a Schengen visa to enter Norway. Here's a breakdown:

- **Visa-Exempt Countries:** Citizens from over 50 countries, including the United States, Canada, Australia, and the United

Kingdom, can enter Norway without a visa for short stays—up to 90 days within a 180-day period. However, starting in 2025, travelers from these visa-exempt countries will need to obtain an ETIAS (European Travel Information and Authorization System) authorization before their trip.

- **ETIAS Authorization:** The ETIAS is a new travel authorization system set to be implemented in 2025. It requires travelers from visa-exempt countries to apply online before their trip. The application process is straightforward, involves a small fee (approximately €7), and the authorization is typically valid for three years or until your passport expires.

- **Visa-Required Countries:** If you're from a country that requires a visa to enter the Schengen Area, you'll need to apply for a Schengen visa before traveling to Norway. This involves submitting an application, providing necessary documentation, and attending an appointment at a Norwegian embassy or consulate.

Passport Validity

Ensure your passport is:

- **Validity**: Valid for at least three months beyond your planned departure date from the Schengen Area.

- **Issue Date:** Issued within the last 10 years.

Customs Regulations

When entering Norway, be aware of customs regulations:

- **Duty-Free Allowances:** You can bring certain quantities of alcohol and tobacco products duty-free. Exceeding these limits may result in taxes or confiscation.

- **Prohibited Items:** Strict regulations apply to the import of meat, dairy products, and plants. It's advisable to avoid bringing these items to prevent issues at customs.

Final Tips

- **Stay Informed:** Entry requirements can change, so always verify the latest information before traveling.

- **Documentation:** Keep all necessary documents, including your passport, ETIAS authorization (if applicable), and any required visas, readily accessible during your journey.

B. Best Time to Visit Norway

Planning your trip to this stunning Scandinavian gem? Let's talk about the best times to visit, so you can experience Norway at its finest.

Summer (June to August)

Summer in Norway is a magical time. From mid-June to mid-August, the country basks in nearly 24 hours of daylight, especially above the Arctic Circle. This phenomenon, known as the Midnight Sun, allows for extended outdoor activities like hiking, fishing, and exploring the fjords. The weather is mild, with temperatures ranging from 13°C to 22°C (55°F to 72°F), making it ideal for sightseeing and enjoying Norway's natural beauty.

Autumn (September to November)

Autumn brings a burst of colors as the landscapes transform into shades of red, orange, and gold. September is particularly pleasant, with cooler temperatures and fewer tourists. It's a great time for hiking and experiencing Norway's cultural festivals. However, by October and November, the weather becomes more unpredictable, with increased rainfall and shorter daylight hours.

Winter (December to February)

If you're a fan of winter activities, Norway doesn't disappoint. From December to February, the country transforms into a snowy paradise. This is the prime time to witness the Northern Lights, especially in Northern Norway. Skiing, dog sledding, and snowmobiling are popular activities during this season. Temperatures can drop significantly, ranging from -6°C to 0°C (21°F to 32°F), so bundle up!

Spring (March to May)

Spring is a time of renewal in Norway. As the snow melts, waterfalls are at their most powerful, and flowers begin to bloom. March and April still offer opportunities for winter sports in higher altitudes, while May brings milder weather and longer days. It's a wonderful time to experience Norway's natural beauty without the summer crowds.

C. Currency, Budgeting, and Costs

Hey there, savvy traveler! Planning your Norwegian adventure? Let's dive into the essentials of currency, budgeting, and costs to help you make the most of your trip without breaking the bank.

Currency in Norway

Norway's official currency is the Norwegian Krone, abbreviated as NOK. As of November 2024, the exchange rate is approximately 1 NOK = 0.08965 USD. Keep in mind that exchange rates fluctuate, so it's wise to check the current rate before your trip.

Budgeting for Your Trip

Norway is known for its high cost of living, but with careful planning, you can enjoy its beauty without overspending. Here's a breakdown of average daily expenses:

- **Accommodation:** A standard 3-star hotel room averages between 1,500 – 1,700 NOK (143 – 162 USD) per night.

- **Meals**: Dining out can be pricey. A meal at a budget restaurant ranges from 170 to 350 NOK, while a three-course meal at a mid-range restaurant can cost between 650 to 1,500 NOK.

- **Transportation:** Public transport is efficient but comes at a cost. A single ticket in Oslo is around 35 NOK, and a 24-hour pass is approximately 105 NOK.

- **Attractions:** Many museums and attractions charge entry fees. For example, the Oslo Pass offers free entry to over 30 museums and unlimited public transport, costing about 445 NOK for a 24-hour pass.

Tips to Save Money

- **Accommodation:** Consider staying in budget-friendly options like hostels or Airbnb. Booking in advance can also secure better rates.

- **Dining:** Save by preparing your own meals or dining at local bakeries and cafes. Supermarkets offer a variety of ready-to-eat options.

- **Transportation:** Utilize public transport passes for unlimited travel within cities. For intercity travel, booking trains and buses in advance can lead to discounts.

- **Attractions:** Take advantage of free attractions like hiking trails, public parks, and certain museums on specific days.

Payment Methods

Credit and debit cards are widely accepted throughout Norway. However, it's advisable to carry some cash for small purchases or in rural areas where card payments might not be available. ATMs are readily accessible in cities and towns.

Tipping Culture

Tipping in Norway is not obligatory. Service charges are typically included in the bill. However, rounding up the bill or leaving a small tip for exceptional service is appreciated.

D. Language and Communication Tips

As you prepare for your adventure, let's talk about language and communication. While many Norwegians speak English, knowing a bit about the local language and cultural nuances can enrich your experience.

Norwegian Language Overview

Norwegian, or "Norsk," is the official language of Norway. It has two written forms: Bokmål and Nynorsk. Bokmål is more widely used, especially in urban areas, while Nynorsk is prevalent in certain regions. Additionally, several minority languages, such as Sami and Kven, are spoken, particularly in the northern regions of the country.

English Proficiency

Norwegians have a high proficiency in English, with more than 80% capable of conversing in the language. In major cities and tourist areas, you'll find that most people, especially younger generations, speak English fluently. This makes it convenient for travelers to communicate without a language barrier.

Basic Norwegian Phrases

While English is widely spoken, learning a few basic Norwegian phrases can enhance your interactions and show respect for the local culture. Here are 10 useful Norwegian phrases in different categories, including their meanings, use cases, and pronunciations:

Essential Norwegian Phrases for Beginners

1. Greetings
- **Phrase**: Hei! (Hi!)
- **Use**: A common, casual greeting when meeting someone.
- **Pronunciation**: [Hey]

2. Introductions
- **Phrase**: Hva heter du? (What's your name?)
- **Use**: Used when you want to ask someone their name.
- **Pronunciation**: [Vah heh-ter doo?]

3. Polite Requests

- **Phrase**: Kan jeg få... ? (Can I have... ?)
- **Use**: A polite way to request something, whether at a restaurant, store, or in any situation.
- **Pronunciation**: [Kahn yay foh...?]

4. **Thanking**
- **Phrase**: Takk så mye! (Thank you very much!)
- **Use**: Used when expressing sincere thanks.
- **Pronunciation**: [Tahk so mee-eh]

5. **Apologizing**
- **Phrase**: Unnskyld! (Excuse me!)
- **Use**: Used when you need to get someone's attention or apologize for a minor inconvenience.
- **Pronunciation**: [Oon-shil]

6. **Asking for Directions**
- **Phrase**: Hvor er... ? (Where is... ?)
- **Use**: Used when asking for directions. You can complete this by adding the location.
- **Pronunciation**: [Vor air...?]

7. **Shopping**
- **Phrase**: Hvor mye koster det? (How much does it cost?)
- **Use**: Used to inquire about the price of something.
- **Pronunciation**: [Vor mee-eh koh-ster deh?]

8. **Traveling**

- **Phrase**: Er dette veien til...? (Is this the way to...?)
- **Use**: Used when asking if you're on the correct path to a destination.
- **Pronunciation**: [Air deh-teh v-eye-en til...?]

9. Ordering Food

- **Phrase**: Jeg vil gjerne ha... (I would like to have...)
- **Use**: A polite way to order food or drinks at a restaurant.
- **Pronunciation**: [Yay vil yah-reh hah...?]

10. Expressing Gratitude for a Gift

- **Phrase**: Tusen takk for gaven! (Thank you so much for the gift!)
- **Use**: When expressing gratitude after receiving a gift.
- **Pronunciation**: [Too-sen tahk for gah-ven]

Cultural Communication Tips

Understanding cultural nuances is key to effective communication in Norway:

- **Directness:** Norwegians value straightforwardness. They appreciate honesty and clarity in conversations.

- **Personal Space:** Respect for personal space is important. Maintain an appropriate distance during conversations and avoid unnecessary physical contact.

- **Non-Verbal Cues:** Maintaining eye contact is considered a sign of attentiveness and sincerity. However, be mindful of facial expressions and gestures, as Norwegians may interpret them differently.

- **Punctuality:** Being on time is highly valued in Norwegian culture. Whether it's a social gathering or a business meeting, punctuality is seen as a sign of respect.

Chapter 4: Planning Your Itinerary

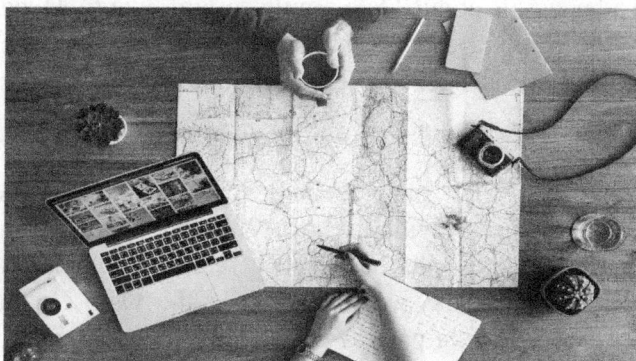

A. 7-Day Classic Norway Experience

Ready to explore Norway in just seven days? This trip is perfect if you want to see the best of what this stunning country has to offer.

Day 1: Hello, Oslo!
Welcome to Norway's capital city! Once you land at Oslo Gardermoen Airport, hop on the express train, and you'll be in the city center in just 20 minutes. Start your day with a walk along the Aker Brygge waterfront, filled with cool shops, restaurants, and stunning views.

In the afternoon, check out the Viking Ship Museum to see real Viking ships up close. It's like stepping back in time! End the day with a delicious seafood dinner at Fjord Restaurant—you can't visit Norway without trying the fish.

Day 2: More Oslo Fun
Today is all about Oslo's culture and beauty. Head to the National Museum to see Edvard Munch's The Scream—it's one of the most famous paintings in the world!

After that, visit the Vigeland Sculpture Park. This place is filled with unique sculptures, and it's a great spot for photos or just relaxing in nature. Wrap up the day with a visit to the Oslo Opera House. The best part? You can walk on its roof for amazing views of the city.

Day 3: The Train Ride of a Lifetime
Get ready for the most scenic train ride ever! Take the Bergen Line from Oslo to Myrdal, and watch as mountains, valleys, and snowy peaks roll by.

At Myrdal, switch to the Flåm Railway, a world-famous ride that takes you past waterfalls and dramatic cliffs. You'll end up in the tiny village of Flåm, where you can relax by the fjord. Grab a drink at the Ægir Brewery—it's got a Viking vibe that's hard to beat!

Day 4: Fjord Cruise and Bergen
This morning, hop on a fjord cruise through the breathtaking Nærøyfjord. Imagine towering cliffs, crystal-clear water, and the sound of waterfalls in the distance. It's pure magic.

After your cruise, make your way to Bergen. Explore the colorful houses at Bryggen Wharf, a UNESCO World Heritage site, and enjoy a fresh seafood dinner at the Fish Market.

Day 5: Bergen's Best
Start your day with a ride on the Fløibanen Funicular to Mount Fløyen. The view from the top is unreal, and there are easy trails if you feel like hiking.

Spend your afternoon exploring Bergen's museums or wandering the cobblestone streets, popping into cute shops and cafes. It's a laid-back day to soak in the charm of this fjord-side city.

Day 6: Hardangerfjord Day Trip
Take a day trip to Hardangerfjord, also known as Norway's fruit basket. Stop by the Steinsdalsfossen Waterfall, where you can walk behind the cascading water (how cool is that?). Try some local cider and enjoy the peaceful scenery before heading back to Bergen.

Day 7: Goodbye, Norway**
Your amazing week in Norway comes to an end today. Depending on your flight, you might have time for one last breakfast or a quick stroll through Bergen. If you're flying out of Oslo, you can take a short flight or hop back on the scenic train.

B. 10-Day Fjord Adventure

Let me show you how to make the most of your 10 days in this stunning country.

Day 1: Arrive in Oslo

Welcome to Oslo! After landing at Oslo Gardermoen Airport, hop on the airport express train to the city center (20 minutes). Spend your day exploring Karl Johans Gate, Oslo's lively main street, filled with shops, cafes, and street performers. End your day with dinner at Fjord Restaurant, where fresh Norwegian seafood takes center stage.

Day 2: Oslo Highlights

Start your morning with a visit to the Viking Ship Museum to learn about Norway's seafaring past. Then, head to the National Museum to see Edvard Munch's The Scream. In the afternoon, visit the Vigeland Sculpture Park, a unique outdoor space with over 200 sculptures. Spend your evening relaxing by the Aker Brygge waterfront with views of Oslo Fjord.

Day 3: Oslo to Flåm

Leave Oslo behind and board the Bergen Line for a train ride filled with spectacular views. At Myrdal, switch to the Flåm Railway, one of the world's most beautiful train journeys. Descend into the charming village of Flåm, surrounded by fjords and mountains. Spend the evening soaking up the scenery with a drink at the Viking-inspired Ægir Brewery.

Day 4: Nærøyfjord Cruise and Aurland
Take a morning fjord cruise through the stunning Nærøyfjord, a UNESCO World Heritage site. Think steep cliffs, peaceful waters, and cascading waterfalls. After your cruise, explore the nearby village of Aurland and visit a local goat farm for some fresh cheese.

Day 5: Bergen
Travel to Bergen, Norway's second-largest city and the perfect base for exploring the fjords. Spend the afternoon wandering through Bryggen Wharf, a colorful row of historic buildings and a UNESCO site. Don't miss the bustling Fish Market, where you can sample fresh seafood.

Day 6: Bergen's Best Views
Start your day with a ride on the Fløibanen Funicular to Mount Fløyen. The panoramic views of Bergen and its surrounding fjords are unforgettable. In the afternoon, visit the KODE Art Museums or take a stroll through the city's cobblestone streets, discovering hidden cafes and boutique shops.

Day 7: Hardangerfjord Day Trip
Head out on a day trip to Hardangerfjord, known as Norway's orchard. Visit the Steinsdalsfossen Waterfall, where you can walk behind the cascading water, and sample local ciders at a nearby farm. Spend the day taking in the tranquil beauty of the fjord before heading back to Bergen.

Day 8: Ålesund
Take a short flight or drive to Ålesund, a coastal town famous for its Art Nouveau architecture. Spend the day exploring its unique buildings and climbing the 418 steps to Aksla Viewpoint for a jaw-dropping view of the city and surrounding islands.

Day 9: Geirangerfjord
Travel to Geirangerfjord, often called Norway's most beautiful fjord. Take a fjord cruise to see famous waterfalls like the Seven Sisters and The Suitor. Hike to nearby viewpoints or visit a local farm for a traditional Norwegian meal.

Day 10: Departure from Ålesund
Your fjord adventure comes to an end. Depending on your flight time, enjoy a peaceful morning in Ålesund before heading to the airport for your journey home.

C. 14-Day Complete Norway Journey
If you're ready to experience the best of Norway, this 14-day itinerary is perfect for you. Packed with fjords, cities, villages, and Arctic wonders, this trip takes you from Oslo to the northernmost reaches of the country.

Day 1: Arrive in Oslo
Welcome to Norway! After landing at Oslo Gardermoen Airport, take the express train to the city center (20 minutes). Spend your afternoon

exploring Aker Brygge, Oslo's waterfront, and enjoying dinner at a local seafood spot.

Day 2: Oslo's Cultural Gems
Dive into Norway's history with a visit to the Viking Ship Museum and the National Museum, home to Edvard Munch's The Scream. End your day with a stroll through Vigeland Sculpture Park.

Day 3: Oslo to Lillehammer
Travel by train to Lillehammer, a charming town known for hosting the 1994 Winter Olympics. Visit the Maihaugen Open-Air Museum and enjoy the town's picturesque setting before settling in for the night.

Day 4: Train to Flåm
Board the Bergen Line to Myrdal, then switch to the Flåm Railway for a jaw-dropping ride to Flåm. Spend the evening exploring the quiet village and enjoying local food at Ægir Brewery.

Day 5: Fjord Cruise and Bergen Arrival
Take a fjord cruise through Nærøyfjord, where towering cliffs and cascading waterfalls surround you. Travel to Bergen in the afternoon and explore the vibrant Bryggen Wharf.

Day 6: Bergen
Start your day with a ride on the Fløibanen Funicular to Mount Fløyen for panoramic views. Spend your afternoon exploring Bergen's museums or walking through its cobblestone streets.

Day 7: Hardangerfjord Adventure
Take a day trip to Hardangerfjord, stopping at Steinsdalsfossen Waterfall. Sample fresh cider and enjoy the peaceful countryside before heading back to Bergen.

Day 8: Ålesund
Fly or drive to Ålesund, a town known for its unique Art Nouveau architecture. Spend the day visiting Aksla Viewpoint and exploring its beautiful streets.

Day 9: Geirangerfjord
Travel to Geirangerfjord, one of Norway's most famous fjords. Take a cruise to see the iconic Seven Sisters Waterfall and hike to nearby viewpoints for stunning photo ops.

Day 10: Trondheim
Head to Trondheim, a city rich in history and charm. Visit the impressive Nidaros Cathedral and enjoy the local food scene.

Day 11: Arctic Circle Adventure
Fly to Bodø, a gateway to the Arctic. Explore the Saltstraumen Maelstrom, the world's strongest tidal current, and enjoy the serene Arctic landscape.

Day 12: Lofoten Islands
Take a ferry to the Lofoten Islands, known for their dramatic peaks and quaint fishing villages. Spend

the day exploring beaches, hiking trails, and picturesque villages like Reine.

Day 13: Tromsø
Fly to Tromsø, where Arctic adventures await. Visit the Arctic Cathedral, take a cable car to Mount Storsteinen, and if it's winter, chase the Northern Lights!

Day 14: Farewell, Norway
Wrap up your journey with a relaxing morning in Tromsø. Depending on your flight schedule, enjoy one last Arctic adventure before heading to the airport for your journey home.

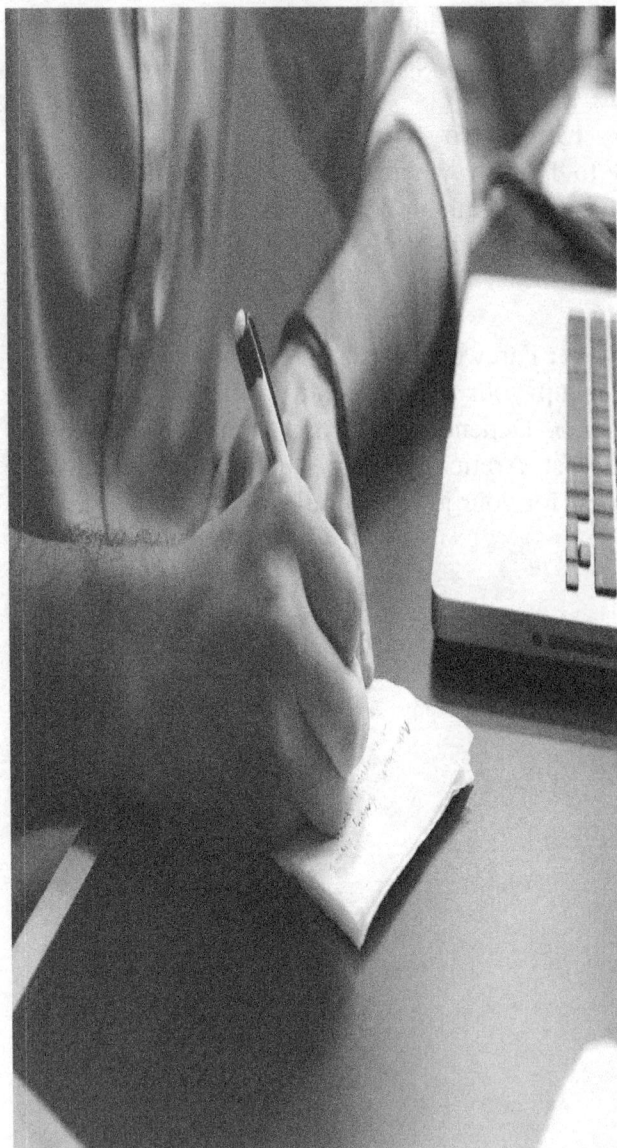

Chapter 5: Norway's Top Destinations

A. Oslo

Welcome to Oslo, the vibrant capital of Norway and the perfect starting point for your adventure. This city isn't just a gateway to fjords and mountains—it's a destination in its own right. Let's dive in!

Do you know where you are?

You're in Oslo, the beating heart of Norway. This city perfectly balances urban energy with a deep connection to nature. One moment, you're exploring cutting-edge architecture; the next, you're hiking in a forest or kayaking in the Oslofjord. It's a place where tradition meets innovation, making it one of the most exciting capitals in Scandinavia.

A Peek into Oslo's History

Oslo's history stretches back over a thousand years, from its founding in 1049 by King Harald Hardrada to its transformation into a cultural and economic hub. The city has survived medieval fires, Danish and Swedish rule, and even WWII occupation. Today, it thrives as a global leader in sustainability, art, and design. With its Viking roots and modern energy, Oslo tells a story you'll want to hear.

Must-See Sights in Oslo

1. The Royal Palace
- **Why You'll Love It:** This stunning 19th-century palace is home to Norway's royal family. Walk through its peaceful gardens and watch the changing of the guard for a touch of royal flair.
- **Good to Know:** Open for guided tours in summer. The gardens are free year-round.

2. The Viking Ship Museum
- **Why You'll Love It:** See actual Viking ships that carried fearless Norsemen across the seas. It's a jaw-dropping glimpse into Norway's legendary past.
- **Good to Know:** Tickets cost around 120 NOK (~$11).

3. Aker Brygge & Tjuvholmen
- **Why You'll Love It:** Oslo's waterfront is packed with trendy restaurants, art galleries,

and stunning fjord views. It's perfect for a sunset stroll or dinner by the water.

4. **Vigeland Sculpture Park**
   - **Why You'll Love It:** With over 200 sculptures, this park is like stepping into an outdoor art gallery. It's peaceful, inspiring, and perfect for photos.
   - **Good to Know:** Free and open 24/7.

5. **The Oslo Opera House**
   - **Why You'll Love It:** This modern masterpiece invites you to literally walk on its roof for panoramic city views. It's an architectural icon and a must-visit spot.

What to Eat in Oslo

Oslo is a food lover's dream. Here's what you shouldn't miss:

   - **Fresh Seafood:** Norway's waters are teeming with delicious fish. Try salmon, cod, or Arctic char at a waterfront restaurant.
   - **Traditional Dishes:** Don't leave without tasting rakfisk (fermented fish) or klippfisk (dried and salted cod).
   - **Cinnamon Buns:** Head to Åpent Bakeri for the best buns in town—soft, sweet, and perfect with coffee.

Outdoor Adventures in Oslo

- **Hike Nordmarka Forest:** Just 20 minutes from downtown, these trails are a green paradise. In winter, it's perfect for cross-country skiing.
- **Kayak the Oslofjord**: Rent a kayak and explore the calm waters, dotted with islands and seaside cabins.

Getting Around Oslo

Public transport in Oslo is top-notch. Grab a 24-hour pass (105 NOK/~$10) for unlimited rides on trams, buses, and ferries. Download the Ruter app for tickets and real-time updates.

Where to Stay

- **Luxury:** The Thief – A stylish hotel in the hip Tjuvholmen area, complete with a rooftop bar and fjord views.
- **Mid-Range:** Scandic Victoria – Comfortable and centrally located, perfect for exploring the city.
- **Budget:** Citybox Oslo – Clean, modern, and wallet-friendly.

B. Bergen

Welcome! You're now in Bergen, the city known for its vibrant Bryggen Wharf, surrounded by seven mountains and stunning fjords. Once a major hub of the Hanseatic League, Bergen combines history, charm, and modern flair. It's also home to Norway's best seafood, making it a paradise for food lovers. With its cozy streets and dramatic landscapes, Bergen feels like a storybook come to life.

A Little Bit of Bergen's History

Founded in 1070, Bergen has a rich maritime history. During the Middle Ages, it was a vital trading port in the Hanseatic League, which brought prosperity and cultural influence to the city. You can still see this history in the Bryggen Wharf, a UNESCO World Heritage site. Today, Bergen is a thriving cultural hub, known for its music festivals, art galleries, and connection to the surrounding fjords.

Must-See Sights in Bergen

1. Bryggen Wharf
- **Why You'll Love It:** This colorful row of wooden houses dates back to the 14th century. It's a photographer's dream and a must-see for history lovers. Wander through the narrow alleyways and imagine what life was like centuries ago.
- **Good to Know:** Many buildings now house shops, cafes, and museums.

2. Fløibanen Funicular
- **Why You'll Love It:** Take a ride to the top of Mount Fløyen for panoramic views of the city, fjords, and mountains. It's a great spot for hiking, picnicking, or just soaking in the scenery.
- **Good to Know:** Tickets cost around 160 NOK (~$15) for a round trip.

3. The Fish Market
- **Why You'll Love It:** This lively market is the perfect place to try fresh seafood, like king crab, salmon, and shrimp. Grab a bite to eat or pick up a unique souvenir.
- **Good to Know:** Open daily, but the best selection is in the morning.

4. Edvard Grieg's Home (Troldhaugen)
- **Why You'll Love It:** Visit the home of Norway's most famous composer, Edvard Grieg. The charming house and concert hall

overlook a peaceful lake, making it a serene escape from the city.

Outdoor Adventures in Bergen

Bergen isn't just about city life—it's also a gateway to some incredible outdoor activities:
- **Hiking**: Trails like Stoltzekleiven and Vidden offer stunning views and are popular with locals.
- **Fjord Cruises:** Hop on a boat tour to explore the nearby fjords, like Hardangerfjord or Sognefjord.

What to Eat in Bergen

Bergen is famous for its fresh, local ingredients. Here are some must-try dishes:
- **Fish Soup:** Creamy and hearty, this soup is a Bergen classic.
- **Seafood Platters:** Treat yourself to a selection of shrimp, crab, and mussels at the Fish Market.
- **Skillingsbolle:** A cinnamon bun that pairs perfectly with a cup of coffee from a local café.

Getting Around Bergen

Bergen is a walkable city, but it also has a reliable public transport system. The Skyss app makes it easy to navigate buses and light rail. A single ticket costs 39 NOK (~$4).

Where to Stay

- **Luxury:** Hotel Norge by Scandic – Modern luxury in the city center with views of the mountains.
- **Mid-Range:** Thon Hotel Rosenkrantz – Comfortable and centrally located, with great breakfast options.
- **Budget:** Bergen Hostel Montana – A friendly and affordable option with easy access to hiking trails.

C. Tromsø

Welcome to Tromsø, the gateway to the Arctic and one of Norway's most magical destinations. Tromsø is like nowhere else. Known as the Gateway to the Arctic, it's a lively city surrounded by snow-covered mountains, fjords, and endless natural beauty. Despite its remote location, Tromsø boasts a vibrant cultural scene, incredible food, and some of the best outdoor adventures you can imagine. Whether you're dog sledding in winter or hiking under the Midnight Sun, Tromsø offers experiences you'll never forget.

A Glimpse into Tromsø's History

Tromsø was established in the 13th century and quickly became an important hub for Arctic exploration. It's been nicknamed the "Paris of the North" due to its bustling trade and surprisingly cosmopolitan vibe. Today, Tromsø is a blend of modernity and tradition, where Arctic expeditions meet cutting-edge science and cozy cafes.

Must-See Attractions in Tromsø

1. The Arctic Cathedral (Ishavskatedralen)
- **Why You'll Love It**: This striking church is one of Tromsø's most iconic landmarks. Its modern architecture, inspired by Arctic ice, is as stunning inside as it is outside.
- **Good to Know:** Attend a Midnight Sun or Northern Lights concert here for a truly magical experience.

2. The Tromsø Cable Car (Fjellheisen)
- **Why You'll Love It:** Take a ride up to Mount Storsteinen for breathtaking views of Tromsø, the fjords, and the surrounding peaks.
- **Good to Know:** Round-trip tickets cost about 250 NOK (~$23). It's especially magical at sunset.

3. Polaria Arctic Experience Center

- **Why You'll Love It**: This quirky, glacier-shaped building houses an Arctic aquarium, interactive exhibits, and films about the region's wildlife and environment. It's perfect for families!

4. Tromsø's Historic City Center

- **Why You'll Love It:** Wander through charming streets lined with colorful wooden houses and explore local shops and cafes. Don't miss Mack Brewery, the northernmost brewery in the world!

Outdoor Adventures in Tromsø

Tromsø is the ultimate destination for Arctic activities:

- **Northern Lights Hunting:** Visit between September and March for the best chance to see this natural wonder. Local guides can take you to the best viewing spots.
- **Dog Sledding:** Glide across snowy landscapes while a team of huskies leads the way.
- **Midnight Sun Hikes:** From May to July, the sun doesn't set. Hike through the stunning Arctic terrain under a golden sky.

What to Eat in Tromsø

Tromsø's food scene is a mix of traditional Arctic flavors and modern cuisine. Must-tries include:

- **Reindeer Stew (Bidos):** A hearty and flavorful Sami dish.
- **Arctic Char**: A local fish that's as fresh as it gets.
- **Cloudberries**: These rare berries are often served with cream or in desserts.

Getting Around Tromsø

Tromsø is compact and easy to navigate. Public buses are reliable, and the Troms Billett app lets you buy tickets (50 NOK/~$5 per ride). Many of the city's attractions are walkable, but taxis and guided tours are also available for reaching more remote spots.

Where to Stay

- **Luxury**: Clarion Hotel The Edge – Stylish, eco-friendly, and located right on the waterfront.
- **Mid-Range:** Scandic Ishavshotel – Comfortable rooms with amazing views of the harbor.
- **Budget:** Tromsø Camping – Cozy cabins surrounded by nature, perfect for outdoor enthusiasts.

D. Stavanger

Welcome to Stavanger, Norway's charming coastal city and the gateway to some of the most dramatic natural wonders in the world. Stavanger is a vibrant city on Norway's southwestern coast, surrounded by fjords, beaches, and rolling hills. It's a hub for oil exploration (earning it the nickname "The Oil Capital of Norway") but also a hotspot for travelers looking to experience Norway's natural beauty. From its lively harbor to its historic old town, Stavanger is a city that welcomes you with open arms.

A Glimpse into Stavanger's History

Stavanger dates back to the Viking Age and became an important religious center in the 12th century with the construction of Stavanger Cathedral. In modern times, it transformed into an oil capital, driving Norway's economic growth. Despite its industrial ties, the city has retained its charm with cobblestone streets, white wooden houses, and a focus on culture and sustainability.

Must-See Attractions in Stavanger

1. Old Stavanger (Gamle Stavanger)
- **Why You'll Love It:** Wander through Europe's best-preserved wooden house district, featuring over 170 white-painted wooden houses from the 18th century. It's like stepping back in time!
- **Good to Know:** Perfect for a leisurely stroll and Instagram-worthy photos.

2. Stavanger Cathedral (Domkirken)
- **Why You'll Love It:** Norway's oldest cathedral, dating back to 1125, is a masterpiece of medieval architecture. Admire its intricate stone carvings and beautiful stained-glass windows.

3. Norwegian Petroleum Museum
- **Why You'll Love It:** Learn about Norway's oil industry in a fun, interactive way. The museum offers a fascinating look at how oil shaped modern Stavanger.
- **Good to Know:** Great for families and curious travelers.

4. Street Art in Stavanger
- **Why You'll Love It:** Stavanger is known for its vibrant street art, with colorful murals and installations scattered throughout the city. Explore on foot and see how art brings the city to life.

Outdoor Adventures Near Stavanger

Stavanger is the perfect base for exploring some of Norway's most iconic natural wonders:

- **Preikestolen (Pulpit Rock):** Hike to this famous cliff that towers 604 meters above Lysefjord. The view will leave you speechless. The hike takes about 4 hours round trip and is suitable for most fitness levels.
- **Kjeragbolten:** For thrill-seekers, hike to this massive boulder wedged between two cliffs. It's a challenging hike but offers unparalleled views.
- **Sola Beach:** Relax on this sandy beach, just a short drive from the city. It's perfect for picnics or a refreshing swim in summer.

What to Eat in Stavanger

Stavanger's food scene is a delightful mix of traditional Norwegian flavors and modern gastronomy. Here's what to try:

- **Lobster and Crab:** Freshly caught and served straight from the sea.
- **Rømmegrøt:** A creamy porridge made with sour cream, perfect for a cozy meal.
- **Local Lamb:** Often served with potatoes and seasonal vegetables, it's a true taste of the region.

Getting Around Stavanger

Stavanger is compact and easy to explore on foot. Public buses connect the city with nearby attractions, and the Kolumbus app is handy for tickets and schedules. For trips to Preikestolen, buses and guided tours are readily available.

Where to Stay

- **Luxury:** Eilert Smith Hotel – A boutique hotel offering stylish rooms and personalized service.
- **Mid-Range:** Clarion Hotel Stavanger – Comfortable and centrally located with a rooftop view.
- **Budget:** Stavanger Bed & Breakfast – A cozy and affordable option for travelers.

E. Trondheim

Welcome to Trondheim, a city steeped in history, charm, and Nordic culture. Trondheim is a vibrant city located in central Norway. Known for its university vibe and rich heritage, it's the third-largest city in the country but feels intimate and welcoming. Surrounded by the stunning Trondheimsfjord, the city is a haven for history buffs, foodies, and anyone who loves a good story.

A Peek into Trondheim's History

Founded in 997 by Viking King Olav Tryggvason, Trondheim was once the capital of Norway. It became an important pilgrimage site during the Middle Ages, with people traveling from across Europe to visit Nidaros Cathedral, built over the tomb of Saint Olav. Today, Trondheim is a modern city that cherishes its historical roots, making it a fascinating place to explore.

Must-See Attractions in Trondheim

1. Nidaros Cathedral
- **Why You'll Love It:** This stunning Gothic cathedral is Norway's national shrine and one of the most important pilgrimage sites in Northern Europe. Marvel at its intricate stonework and climb the tower for panoramic city views.
- **Good to Know**: Guided tours are available, and tickets cost around 120 NOK (~$11).

2. Gamle Bybro (The Old Town Bridge)
- **Why You'll Love It:** Known as "The Gateway to Happiness," this iconic red

bridge offers beautiful views of the colorful wooden houses along the Nidelva River.

- **Good to Know:** Don't forget to snap a photo—it's one of Trondheim's most Instagrammable spots!

3. Bakklandet

- **Why You'll Love It:** This charming district is filled with cobblestone streets, cozy cafes, and historic wooden houses. It's the perfect place to enjoy a leisurely stroll or a cup of coffee by the river.

4. Ringve Music Museum

- **Why You'll Love It:** Explore Norway's musical history at this fascinating museum located in a beautiful 18th-century manor house.

Outdoor Adventures in Trondheim

Trondheim isn't just about history—it's also a gateway to incredible outdoor experiences:
Kayaking on the Nidelva River: Paddle through the heart of the city and take in the views from the water.

- **Hiking in Bymarka:** Just outside the city, this nature reserve offers peaceful trails, lakes, and scenic viewpoints.

What to Eat in Trondheim

Trondheim has a vibrant food scene that emphasizes local and seasonal ingredients. Here are some must-try dishes:

- **Klippfisk:** Dried and salted cod, prepared in traditional Norwegian style.
- **Sodd:** A hearty lamb and vegetable soup, perfect for chilly days.
- **Cinnamon Buns:** The bakeries here make some of the best in Norway!

For a special treat, book a table at Credo, a Michelin-starred restaurant that highlights sustainable Norwegian cuisine.

Getting Around Trondheim

Trondheim is a walkable city, but its public transport system, operated by AtB, makes it easy to get around. Single tickets cost about 40 NOK (~$4), and you can use the AtB app to plan your trips.

Where to Stay

- **Luxury:** Britannia Hotel – A historic, five-star hotel with modern amenities and a luxurious spa.
- **Mid-Range:** Thon Hotel Nidaros – Comfortable and centrally located with great breakfast options.
- **Budget:** Trondheim Vandrerhjem Hostel – Affordable, clean, and ideal for budget travelers.

F. The Lofoten Islands

The Lofoten Islands are a cluster of rugged islands located above the Arctic Circle. Known for their sharp, dramatic mountains rising from crystal-clear waters, this region is a photographer's dream. From midnight sun in the summer to dancing Northern Lights in winter, the Lofoten Islands are a year-round wonder.

A Bit of History

The Lofoten Islands have been inhabited for thousands of years, with roots in Viking history and a strong connection to fishing. Cod fishing has been the backbone of life here for centuries, and you can still see traditional drying racks for stockfish lining the shores. Today, the islands are a blend of ancient traditions and a thriving tourism industry that celebrates their natural beauty.

Must-See Attractions in the Lofoten Islands

1. Reine:

- **Why You'll Love It:** This postcard-perfect fishing village is surrounded by towering peaks and shimmering fjords. Stroll through its colorful streets and soak in the views.
- **Good to Know:** Reine is a great base for exploring nearby hiking trails and kayaking spots.

2. Hamnøy:
- **Why You'll Love It:** Hamnøy is home to some of the most iconic views of the Lofoten Islands, with red cabins perched on rocky shores against a backdrop of jagged peaks.

3. Kvalvika Beach
- **Why You'll Love It:** This secluded beach is only accessible via a scenic hike. Imagine soft golden sand surrounded by mountains—it's a peaceful slice of paradise.
- **Good to Know:** The hike takes about 2-3 hours round trip, so bring sturdy shoes and water.

4. Lofotr Viking Museum
- **Why You'll Love It**: Step back in time at this living museum, where you can learn about Viking history, explore a reconstructed longhouse, and even try axe throwing!

Outdoor Adventures in the Lofoten Islands

This region is an outdoor enthusiast's paradise:

- **Hiking:** Trails like Ryten and Munkebu offer breathtaking views of mountains and fjords.
- **Fishing:** Try your hand at cod fishing, a tradition that has shaped life in Lofoten for centuries.
- **Kayaking:** Paddle through calm waters surrounded by dramatic cliffs and wildlife.

What to Eat in the Lofoten Islands

The Lofoten Islands are known for their fresh, local flavors. Must-tries include:
- **Stockfish:** Dried cod, a traditional Arctic delicacy that's been a staple here for centuries.
- **Arctic Char:** A light, flavorful fish often served grilled or smoked.
- **Brunost (Brown Cheese):** A sweet, caramel-like cheese that pairs perfectly with freshly baked bread.

Getting Around the Lofoten Islands

Renting a car is the best way to explore the islands at your own pace. The E10 Highway connects most of the major villages, making it easy to navigate. Public buses are available but infrequent, so plan accordingly.

Where to Stay

- **Luxury:** Svinøya Rorbuer – Stay in a traditional fisherman's cabin with modern comforts and stunning waterfront views.
- **Mid-Range:** Eliassen Rorbuer – Cozy cabins in Hamnøy with easy access to scenic spots.
- **Budget:** Lofoten Vandrerhjem Hostel – An affordable, friendly option perfect for solo travelers or groups.

G. Svalbard

Welcome to Svalbard, the northernmost inhabited place on Earth. If you're ready for an unforgettable adventure in the Arctic, this is the destination for you. Svalbard is a group of islands located halfway between mainland Norway and the North Pole. The largest settlement, Longyearbyen, is your gateway to this Arctic paradise. Despite its remote location, Svalbard is a bustling hub of activity, offering a mix of outdoor adventures, cozy lodges, and fascinating cultural experiences.

A Bit of History

The name "Svalbard" means "cold coasts" in Old Norse, and it was first mentioned in Viking records from 1194. The islands were rediscovered by Dutch explorers in the 16th century and later became a hub for whaling, mining, and Arctic exploration. Today, Svalbard is governed by Norway and remains a center for scientific research and eco-tourism.

Must-See Attractions in Svalbard

1. Longyearbyen:
- **Why You'll Love It:** This charming settlement is the heart of Svalbard, with colorful houses, museums, and a surprising range of restaurants and cafes. Explore the Svalbard Museum to learn about the islands' history and wildlife.

2. Isfjord Radio Station
- **Why You'll Love It:** A remote outpost turned boutique hotel, this spot offers breathtaking views of the Arctic wilderness. It's perfect for unwinding after a day of adventure.

3. Nordenskiöld Glacier
- **Why You'll Love It:** One of Svalbard's most iconic glaciers, this is a great spot for guided glacier hikes or kayaking trips. Its icy blue beauty is unforgettable.

4. Pyramiden: The Ghost Town

- **Why You'll Love It**: Once a thriving Soviet mining town, Pyramiden is now a fascinating ghost town. Take a guided tour to explore its eerie charm and learn about its unique history.

Outdoor Adventures in Svalbard

Svalbard is a haven for outdoor enthusiasts:
- **Dog Sledding:** Glide through snowy landscapes with a team of eager huskies.
- **Snowmobiling:** Explore vast Arctic tundras and frozen fjords.
- **Wildlife Safaris:** Spot polar bears, Arctic foxes, and seals in their natural habitat.
- **Northern Lights**: Visit between November and February for the chance to see the Aurora Borealis dance across the sky.

What to Eat in Svalbard

Despite its remote location, Svalbard offers incredible dining experiences:
- **Reindeer Steak:** A tender, flavorful meat that's a local favorite.
- **Arctic Char:** A light, flaky fish that's caught fresh from the icy waters.
- **Cloudberry Desserts**: These rare berries are a sweet Arctic treat, often served with cream.

For a unique experience, dine at Huset, one of the northernmost fine dining restaurants in the world. Its Arctic-inspired menu is a must-try.

Getting Around Svalbard

Longyearbyen is small and easy to explore on foot. For adventures outside the settlement, guided tours and snowmobiles are the way to go. Remember, polar bears roam freely here, so traveling with a guide is essential for safety.

Where to Stay

- **Luxury:** Funken Lodge – A cozy, elegant lodge with stunning views and top-notch dining.
- **Mid-Range:** Radisson Blu Polar Hotel – The world's northernmost full-service hotel, offering comfort and convenience.
- **Budget:** Gjestehuset 102 – A simple and friendly guesthouse ideal for budget-conscious travelers.

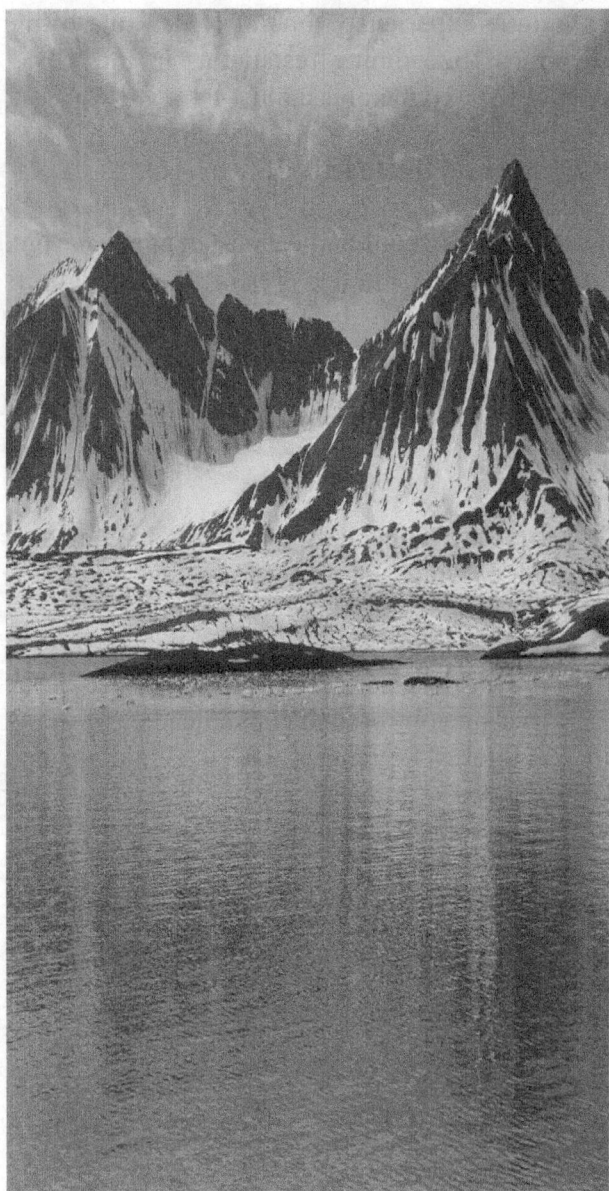

Chapter 6: Norway's Natural Wonders

A. Fjords of Norway

Let's explore why these natural wonders are a must-see on your journey.

What Are Fjords?

Fjords are deep, narrow inlets of the sea carved by glaciers during the Ice Age. Norway is blessed with over 1,000 of them, making it one of the best places in the world to experience their grandeur. Each fjord has its own unique beauty, from serene waters and lush greenery to dramatic cliffs and snow-capped peaks.

The Most Iconic Fjords of Norway

1. Geirangerfjord
- **Why You'll Love It:** This UNESCO World Heritage site is famous for its emerald-green

waters, majestic cliffs, and iconic waterfalls like the Seven Sisters and The Suitor.

- **What to Do:** Take a fjord cruise for up-close views of the waterfalls or hike to viewpoints like Dalsnibba for a bird's-eye perspective.

2. **Nærøyfjord:**
   - **Why You'll Love It:** Another UNESCO site, Nærøyfjord is known for its narrow passageways and peaceful atmosphere. Surrounded by steep mountains, it's a true slice of serenity.
   - **What to Do:** Kayak through its calm waters or enjoy a ferry ride from Gudvangen to Flåm.

3. **Hardangerfjord:**
   - **Why You'll Love It:** Hardangerfjord is famous for its fruit orchards, especially during spring when the blossoms are in full bloom. It's also home to the spectacular Vøringsfossen Waterfall.
   - **What to Do:** Visit a local cider farm, hike the Trolltunga, or simply enjoy the scenic drive along the fjord.

4. **Sognefjord:**
   - **Why You'll Love It:** At over 200 kilometers long, Sognefjord is Norway's largest and deepest fjord. Its sheer scale and beauty are awe-inspiring.

- **What to Do:** Explore charming villages like Balestrand and take a RIB boat tour for a thrilling ride through the fjord.

How to Experience Norway's Fjords

1. Fjord Cruises
A cruise is one of the best ways to take in the grandeur of the fjords. Opt for popular routes like Flåm to Gudvangen or multi-day journeys with Hurtigruten Coastal Express.

2. Hiking
Norway's fjords are surrounded by incredible hiking trails. Some of the most famous include:
- **Trolltunga:** A challenging hike with a breathtaking reward.
- **Pulpit Rock (Preikestolen):** A relatively easier hike with jaw-dropping views.
- **Romsdalseggen Ridge:** One of the most scenic hikes in Norway.

3. Kayaking
Paddle through the calm waters of fjords like Nærøyfjord or Geirangerfjord for a peaceful and up-close experience.

4. Driving
Scenic routes like the Hardanger Scenic Drive or the roads along Sognefjord offer breathtaking vistas around every corner.

Best Time to Visit the Fjords

- **Spring (April to June):** Waterfalls are at their fullest, and fruit orchards are in bloom.
- **Summer (June to August):** Long daylight hours and warmer weather make this the best time for hiking and cruises.
- **Autumn (September to October):** The fjords are quieter, and the fall colors add a magical touch.
- **Winter (November to March):** Snowy landscapes and fewer crowds make it perfect for a peaceful retreat.

B. Northern Lights

Have you ever dreamed of seeing the sky come alive with swirling colors of green, purple, and pink? Norway is one of the best places in the world to experience the Northern Lights, or Aurora Borealis, a natural phenomenon that feels nothing short of magical. Let's dive into where, when, and how to catch this breathtaking Arctic light show!

What Are the Northern Lights?

The Northern Lights are caused by solar particles colliding with Earth's magnetic field, creating vibrant ribbons of light that dance across the polar skies. This natural wonder has inspired myths and stories for centuries, and seeing it in person is an experience you'll never forget.

Where to See the Northern Lights in Norway

1. Tromsø:

- **Why It's Awesome:** Tromsø is often called the "Gateway to the Arctic," and its location above the Arctic Circle makes it one of the top spots for Northern Lights viewing.
- **What to Do:** Join a guided tour to escape city lights, or take the Tromsø Cable Car to watch the auroras from Mount Storsteinen.

2. Svalbard:

- **Why It's Awesome:** Svalbard, located halfway between mainland Norway and the North Pole, offers some of the darkest skies in the world. Here, you can even see the lights during the day in the polar night season!
- **What to Do:** Take a snowmobile safari or dog sledding tour to chase the lights in this remote Arctic wonderland.

3. Lofoten Islands: Nature's Masterpiece

- **Why It's Awesome:** The Lofoten Islands combine dramatic landscapes with incredible aurora displays. Imagine watching the lights reflect on calm fjord waters or illuminate sharp mountain peaks.

- **What to Do:** Rent a cozy rorbuer (fishing cabin) and enjoy the lights from your doorstep.

4. Alta:

- **Why It's Awesome:** Known as the "City of the Northern Lights," Alta has a rich history of aurora research and a great chance of sightings.
- **What to Do:** Visit the Northern Lights Cathedral or stay in the Sorrisniva Igloo Hotel for a unique Arctic experience.

When to See the Northern Lights in Norway

The best time to see the Northern Lights is between September and March, when the nights are longest and the skies are darkest. Here's a quick guide:

- **September-October:** The aurora season begins, and the weather is milder.
- **November-January**: Peak aurora time with long, dark nights. Polar nights in northern regions mean 24-hour darkness.
- **February-March:** Clear skies and slightly warmer temperatures make this a popular time for aurora hunting.

How to Maximize Your Chances

1. Find Dark Skies
   Light pollution can drown out the auroras, so head to remote locations away from city lights. Guided tours are great for finding the best spots.

2. Check the Weather
   Clear skies are essential. Use apps like YR.no to check cloud cover in advance.

3. Be Patient
   The Northern Lights are unpredictable, so be prepared to wait. Dress warmly, bring snacks, and enjoy the stars while you wait for the show to begin.

4. Use Aurora Forecasts
   Websites like Aurora Service and apps like My Aurora Forecast help you track aurora activity and predict the best times to see them.

Aurora-Friendly Activities

While you wait for the lights to appear, why not add some Arctic adventures to your trip?
- **Dog Sledding:** Glide across snowy landscapes under the stars.
- **Snowmobiling**: A thrilling way to explore the Arctic wilderness.
- **Reindeer Encounters:** Learn about Sami culture and meet these gentle creatures.

What to Bring for Aurora Watching

- **Warm Clothes**: Layers are essential in Arctic temperatures. Don't forget gloves, hats, and thermal socks.
- **Camera and Tripod:** The Northern Lights are tricky to capture, so bring a good camera and practice long-exposure shots.
- **Snacks and Hot Drinks:** Staying warm and cozy makes the experience even better.

C. Midnight Sun

Imagine a world where the sun doesn't set, where golden light bathes the land at midnight, and you feel like you've stepped into a dream. Welcome to Norway during the Midnight Sun! This natural phenomenon, found in the Arctic Circle, is an unforgettable experience that turns night into day and fills the air with an endless sense of wonder. Let's explore what makes the Midnight Sun so special and how you can experience it for yourself.

What Is the Midnight Sun?

The Midnight Sun is a natural phenomenon where the sun remains visible for 24 hours a day. This happens during the summer months in areas above the Arctic Circle, such as northern Norway. It's caused by the Earth's tilt, which allows the sun to stay above the horizon even at night. The result? A surreal, golden glow that never fades.

Where to Experience the Midnight Sun in Norway

1. Tromsø:
- **Why It's Awesome:** Tromsø is a popular spot for experiencing the Midnight Sun, thanks to its vibrant atmosphere and easy access to Arctic nature. Hike to Mount Storsteinen or take a Midnight Sun cruise for the best views.
- **When to See It**: From May 20 to July 22.

2. Svalbard:
- **Why It's Awesome:** In Svalbard, the Midnight Sun lasts from late April to late August, making it one of the longest Midnight Sun periods in Norway. Enjoy activities like kayaking, glacier hiking, and wildlife safaris under the golden Arctic light.
- **When to See It:** From April 20 to August 22.

3. The Lofoten Islands:

- **Why It's Awesome:** The rugged peaks and calm waters of the Lofoten Islands make for stunning Midnight Sun photography. Watch the sun dip low on the horizon without ever setting—it's pure magic.
- **When to See It:** From May 27 to July 17.

4. Nordkapp (North Cape):
- **Why It's Awesome**: Standing at the North Cape, the northernmost point in Europe, is an awe-inspiring way to experience the Midnight Sun. The vast ocean views make this spot feel like the edge of the world.
- **When to See It:** From May 14 to July 29.

What to Do Under the Midnight Sun

1. Hiking
Explore trails like Ryten in the Lofoten Islands or Fjellheisen in Tromsø for surreal views at midnight.

2. Midnight Sun Cruises
Sail through the calm Arctic waters as the golden sun casts its glow over fjords, cliffs, and wildlife.

3. Kayaking
Paddle through crystal-clear waters under a sky that never darkens.

4. Fishing
Take part in Norway's rich fishing tradition and try your hand at catching cod, halibut, or Arctic char.

5. Wildlife Watching
Look for reindeer, Arctic foxes, and seabirds, all active during the Midnight Sun.

Tips for Enjoying the Midnight Sun

- **Pack an Eye Mask:** The constant daylight can be disorienting for sleep, so bring an eye mask to help you rest.
- **Embrace the Energy:** The Midnight Sun is energizing—use it to explore and make the most of the long days.
- **Capture the Moment:** Bring a camera to photograph the unique light. The soft, golden glow makes everything look magical.

Best Time to Visit for the Midnight Sun

The Midnight Sun occurs between May and August in Norway, with exact dates depending on the location. The further north you go, the longer the Midnight Sun lasts. Plan your trip during this period to experience the phenomenon in full effect.

D. Norway's National Parks

Hello ! Let's explore some of the country's most incredible national parks and discover why they're a must-visit for any traveler!

What Makes Norway's National Parks Special?

Norway is home to 47 national parks, each offering unique ecosystems and spectacular scenery. These parks showcase the country's natural diversity, from Arctic tundras to lush forests and glacial valleys. They're not just places to visit—they're places to experience.

Norway's Top National Parks

1. Jotunheimen National Park
- **Why You'll Love It:** Known as the "Home of the Giants," Jotunheimen is famous for its rugged peaks, including Galdhøpiggen, the highest mountain in Northern Europe. This park is a hiker's paradise with over 250 mountain trails.

What to Do:

- Take on the iconic Besseggen Ridge Hike for jaw-dropping views.
- Visit Gjende Lake, known for its striking turquoise waters.
- Spot reindeer and golden eagles in their natural habitat.

2. Rondane National Park
- **Why You'll Love It:** As Norway's oldest national park, Rondane is a peaceful escape filled with rolling hills, alpine lakes, and ten majestic peaks over 2,000 meters.

What to Do:
- Hike to Rondslottet, the park's highest peak.
- Go horseback riding along scenic trails.
- Camp under the stars for a true wilderness experience.

3. Hardangervidda National Park
- **Why You'll Love It:** Europe's largest mountain plateau, Hardangervidda, offers vast, open landscapes perfect for hiking and cross-country skiing. It's also home to one of the largest herds of wild reindeer in Europe.

What to Do:
- Explore the Hardangervidda Trail, a multi-day trek with cozy cabins along the way.
- Visit Vøringsfossen Waterfall, one of Norway's most spectacular cascades.

4. Dovrefjell-Sunndalsfjella National Park

- **Why You'll Love It:** This park is famous for its population of wild musk oxen. The rugged mountains and lush valleys also make it a favorite for hiking and wildlife photography.

What to Do:

- Join a guided musk ox safari to see these prehistoric creatures up close.
- Hike to Snøhetta, the park's highest peak, for panoramic views.

5. Lofotodden National Park

- **Why You'll Love It:** Located in the Lofoten Islands, this park combines dramatic cliffs, white sandy beaches, and crystal-clear waters. It's a paradise for photographers and adventurers.

What to Do:

- Hike to Ryten for views of Kvalvika Beach.
- Explore hidden coves and kayak along the coastline.

Wildlife in Norway's National Parks

Norway's parks are teeming with wildlife, offering incredible opportunities to see animals in their natural habitats:

- **Reindeer:** Found in parks like Hardangervidda and Rondane.
- **Musk Oxen:** Spot these ancient animals in Dovrefjell-Sunndalsfjella.
- **Arctic Foxes:** Rare but occasionally seen in northern parks like Varangerhalvøya.

- **Golden Eagles and Sea Eagles:** Common in mountainous and coastal parks.

Tips for Exploring Norway's National Parks

1. Plan Ahead
Norway's parks are vast, so research your routes and pack appropriately.

2. Dress for the Weather
Weather can change quickly, especially in the mountains. Wear layers and waterproof gear.

3. Respect Nature
Follow the Leave No Trace principles to preserve Norway's pristine wilderness.

4. Stay in Cabins
Norway's parks are dotted with cozy mountain cabins (called DNT huts) that make overnight hikes comfortable and memorable.

Best Time to Visit

- **Summer (June to August):** Perfect for hiking, with long daylight hours and warmer weather.
- **Autumn (September to October):** Enjoy fewer crowds and stunning fall foliage.
- **Winter (November to March):** Ideal for skiing and snowshoeing adventures.

- **Spring (April to May):** Watch as the landscape awakens with blooming flowers and flowing rivers.

E. Iconic Road Trips

Buckle up, and let's explore these scenic drives that will leave you spellbound!

1. Trollstigen:
- **Why It's Iconic:** Trollstigen, or "The Troll's Path," is a jaw-dropping mountain road with 11 hairpin bends and a 9% incline. Surrounded by dramatic peaks and cascading waterfalls, it's one of Norway's most famous drives.

What to Do:
- Stop at the Trollstigen Viewpoint, a cantilevered platform offering panoramic views of the winding road below.
- Visit Stigfossen Waterfall, which thunders down the mountainside and runs under the road.

Best Time to Visit: Open from late May to October, depending on weather.

Good to Know: The road can get busy in summer, so visit early in the day for a quieter experience.

2. Atlantic Road:
- **Why It's Iconic:** Often called "The World's Most Beautiful Road," the Atlantic Road links a series of small islands with sweeping bridges and causeways. Driving here feels

like gliding over the ocean, especially during high waves or stormy weather.

What to Do:

- Stop at Storseisundet Bridge, the most famous and photogenic of the bridges.
- Pack a picnic and enjoy it at one of the roadside rest areas with ocean views.
- Try fishing off the roadside platforms, a unique Atlantic Road experience.

Best Time to Visit: Open year-round, but especially dramatic during autumn storms.

3. Geiranger-Trollstigen National Tourist Route

- **Why It's Iconic:** This route combines two of Norway's most spectacular attractions: the Geirangerfjord and Trollstigen. Winding through fjords, mountains, and valleys, it's a must-do for nature lovers.

What to Do:

- Drive to the Eagle's Bend Viewpoint for sweeping views of Geirangerfjord.
- Stop at Ørnesvingen and Flydalsjuvet, iconic viewpoints with breathtaking photo opportunities.

Best Time to Visit: Summer and early autumn offer the best weather for this route.

4. Hardanger Scenic Route:

- **Why It's Iconic:** This road hugs the edge of the stunning Hardangerfjord, taking you through orchards, quaint villages, and past roaring waterfalls like Vøringsfossen.

What to Do:

- Visit Steinsdalsfossen, a waterfall you can walk behind.
- Stop at a local cider farm to taste Hardanger's famous apple ciders.

Best Time to Visit: Spring, when the orchards are in full bloom, or autumn for vibrant fall colors.

5. Sognefjellet National Tourist Route:
Why It's Iconic: As Northern Europe's highest mountain pass, this route offers a unique mix of snow-capped peaks, glaciers, and alpine lakes.
What to Do:
- Stop at Fantesteinen, the highest point of the route, for spectacular views.
- Visit the Jotunheimen National Park for hiking trails leading into Norway's wild heart.

Best Time to Visit: Open from May to September, when the snow has melted.

6. Helgeland Coastal Route:
- **Why It's Iconic:** This less-traveled route along Norway's northern coast offers pristine beaches, rugged islands, and the chance to cross the Arctic Circle.

What to Do:
- Take a ferry to the Vega Archipelago, a UNESCO World Heritage site.
- Stop by the Torghatten Mountain, known for its unique hole through the middle.

Best Time to Visit: Summer, for warmer weather and endless daylight.

Tips for Road Tripping in Norway

1. Plan Your Stops
Norway's roads are filled with viewpoints, rest areas, and hiking trails. Plan for plenty of stops to take it all in.

2. Drive Carefully
The roads can be narrow and winding, especially in mountainous areas. Take your time and enjoy the views.

3. Pack Snacks and Drinks
Some stretches of road are remote, so it's good to have refreshments on hand.

4. Check the Weather
Conditions can change quickly, especially in the mountains. Make sure your car is equipped for the season.

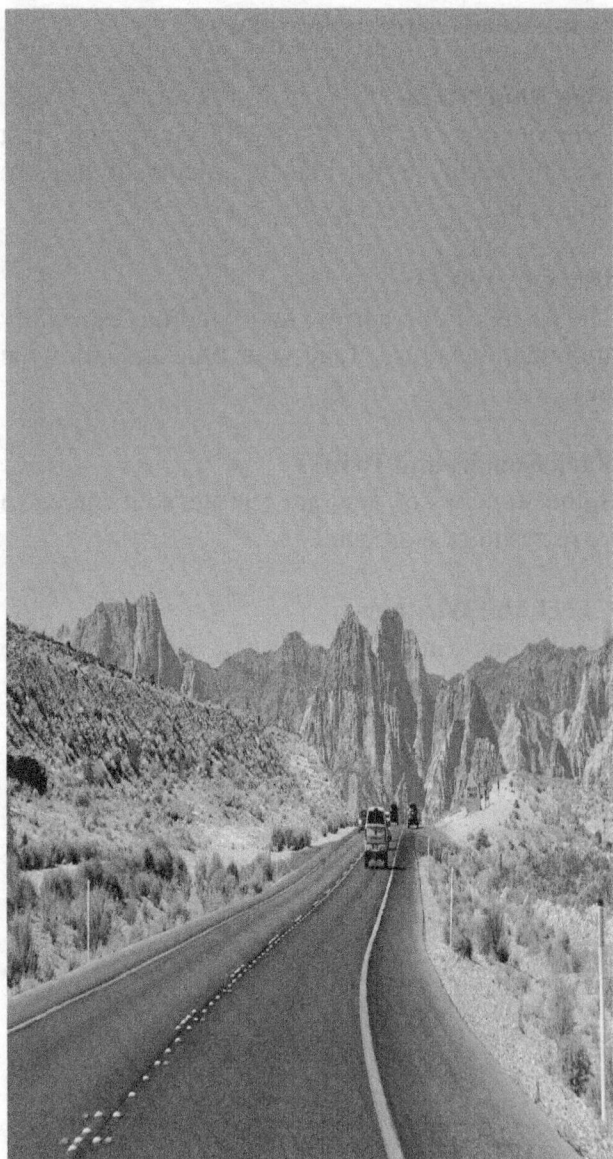

Chapter 7:
Accommodation

A. Luxury Hotels You Should Consider

If you're looking for the ultimate in luxury, these are the hotels you should consider.

1. The Grand Hotel Oslo

The Grand Hotel Oslo

Grand Hotel Oslo
Karl Johans gt. 31, 0159 Oslo, Norway

4.4 ★★★★★

View larger map

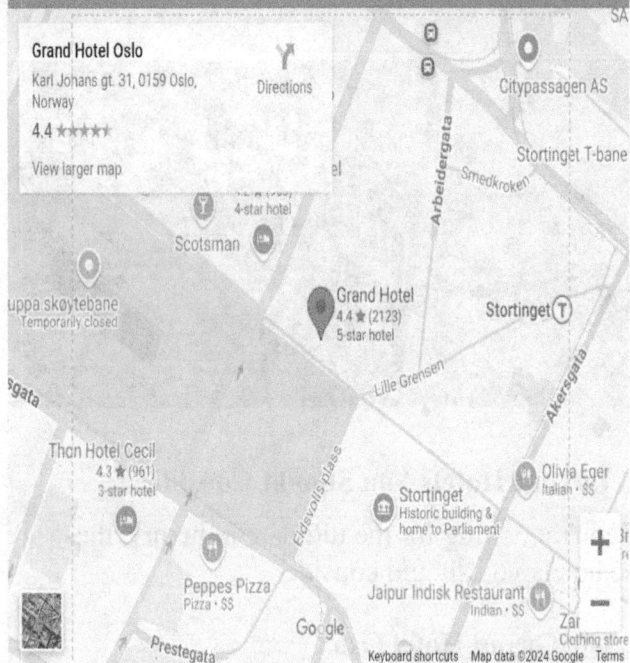

Directions

Citypassagen AS

Stortinget T-bane

Arbeidergata

Smedkroken

4-star hotel

Scotsman

uppa skøytebane
Temporarily closed

Grand Hotel
4.4 ★ (2123)
5-star hotel

Stortinget (T)

Akersgata

Lille Grensen

sgata

Than Hotel Cecil
4.3 ★ (961)
3-star hotel

Eidsvolls plass

Stortinget
Historic building &
home to Parliament

Olivia Eger
Italian · $$

Peppes Pizza
Pizza · $$

Jaipur Indisk Restaurant
Indian · $$

Zar
Clothing store

Google

Prestegata

Keyboard shortcuts   Map data ©2024 Google   Terms

SCAN THE QR CODE

1. Open your device camera app.
2. Position the QR code in the camera frame.
3. Hold your phone steady.
4. Wait for the code to be recognized.
5. Once recognized, tap on the notification or follow the prompt to access the content or action associated with the Qr code

Location: Oslo, Norway

Situated in the heart of Oslo, The Grand Hotel is an iconic landmark that has welcomed royalty, politicians, and celebrities for over a century. First opened in 1874, this elegant hotel combines classic charm with modern luxury. With its central location, you're just steps away from Oslo's main attractions, such as the National Opera House, Karl Johans gate, and the Royal Palace.

What's Special: The Grand Hotel is known for its stunning view of the Oslo fjord from the rooftop terrace. It also boasts a world-class spa, perfect for a relaxing retreat after a busy day. The blend of traditional Norwegian craftsmanship with contemporary design makes this hotel feel both timeless and modern.

Price: Rooms range from $250 to $500 per night, depending on the season and type of room.

How to Book: Visit the hotel's official website www.grand.no or call +47 23 21 20 00 for reservations.

Opening Times: Open year-round.

2. Hotel Continental

Hotel Continental

Hotel Continental, Oslo

Stortingsgata 24/26, 0117 Oslo, Norway

Directions

4.6 ★★★★★

View larger map

SCAN THE QR CODE

1. Open your device camera app.
2. Position the QR code in the camera frame.
3. Hold your phone steady.
4. Wait for the code to be recognized.
5. Once recognized, tap on the notification or follow the prompt to access the content or action associated with the Qr code

Location: Oslo, Norway

If you're searching for the perfect mix of elegance, luxury, and history, Hotel Continental is the place to be. Opened in 1900, this family-owned hotel is located in the heart of Oslo, near the famous National Theatre and the Aker Brygge district. It has long been the choice of Norwegian royalty and dignitaries.

What's Special: Hotel Continental is known for its impeccable service, timeless décor, and spacious rooms that provide stunning views of the city's waterfront. The on-site Theatercaféen, a classic Oslo dining experience, is a must-visit for both tourists and locals alike.

Price: Rooms start from $300 per night.

How to Book: You can book online at www.continental.oslo.no or by calling +47 23 10 30 00.

Opening Times: Open year-round.

3. Norefjell Ski & Resort

Norefjell Ski & Resort

Norefjell
Norefjell, Norefjellveien 927, 3536
Noresund, Norway
4.5 ★★★★★
View larger map

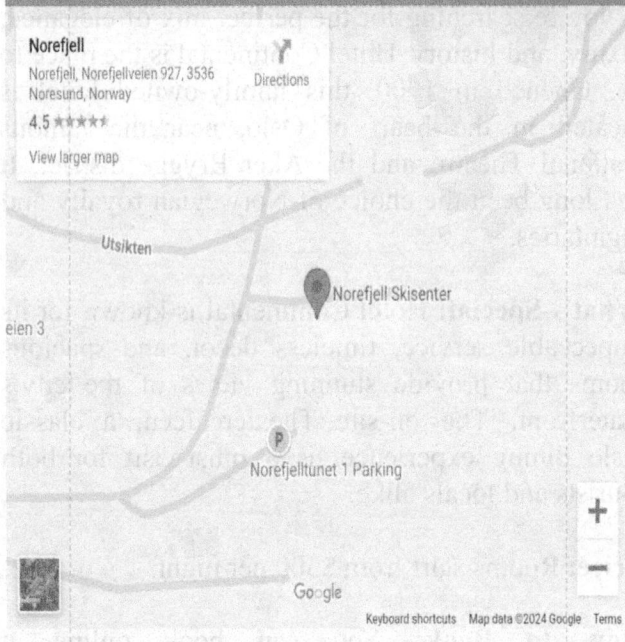

Utsikten

eien 3

Norefjell Skisenter

P
Norefjelltunet 1 Parking

+
−

Google
Keyboard shortcuts   Map data ©2024 Google   Terms

SCAN THE QR CODE

1. Open your device camera app.
2. Position the QR code in the camera frame.
3. Hold your phone steady.
4. Wait for the code to be recognized.
5. Once recognized, tap on the notification or follow the prompt to access the content or action associated with the Qr code

Location: Krødsherad, Norway (near Lake Krøderen)

For a blend of luxury and adventure, Norefjell Ski & Resort is an incredible option. Located just 80 kilometers from Oslo, this resort offers a perfect escape into the Norwegian mountains. Whether you're into skiing, hiking, or simply enjoying the crisp mountain air, Norefjell has it all. It's a great choice for travelers looking for a winter wonderland experience, especially during the ski season.

What's Special: The hotel's unique location on the mountainside offers incredible panoramic views of the surrounding nature. After a day on the slopes, you can relax in the resort's sauna or enjoy a gourmet meal at the on-site restaurant, overlooking the beautiful fjord.

Price: Prices vary by season, with rates starting at $220 per night.

How to Book: Book via www.norefjell.com or call +47 32 07 73 00.

Opening Times: Open year-round, with peak seasons in winter and summer.

4. The Thief

The Thief

THE THIEF
Landgangen 1, 0252 Oslo, Norway

Directions

4.4 ★★★★★

View larger map

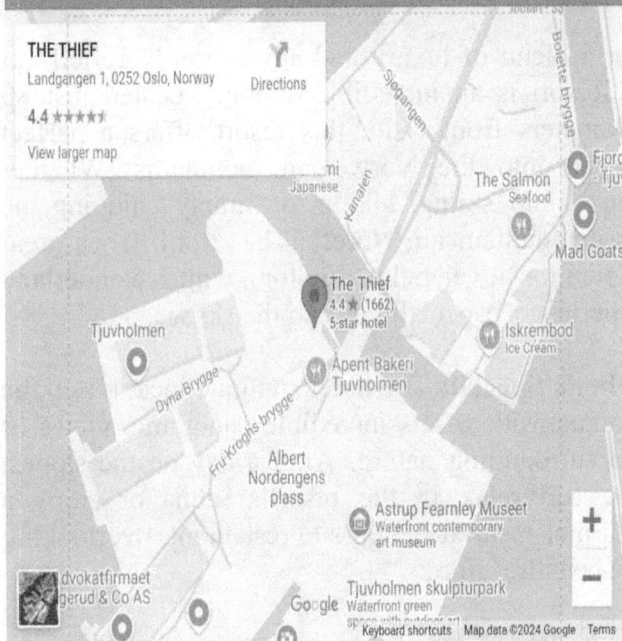

SCAN THE QR CODE

1. Open your device camera app.

2. Position the QR code in the camera frame.

3. Hold your phone steady.

4. Wait for the code to be recognized.

5. Once recognized, tap on the notification or follow the prompt to access the content or action associated with the Qr code

Location: Oslo, Norway (Aker Brygge district)

Named after a local criminal who was said to have stolen the "thief's treasure," The Thief is a modern and stylish hotel located in Oslo's trendy Aker Brygge district. This five-star hotel is as much a work of art as it is a place to stay. With a focus on contemporary design, it's a favorite among art lovers and luxury travelers alike.

What's Special: The Thief boasts an extensive collection of modern art, which adds a creative touch to every corner of the hotel. Its luxurious rooms offer stunning views of the Oslo fjord, and the rooftop bar provides an ideal setting for watching the sunset over the water.

Price: Rates start around $350 per night.

How to Book: Visit www.thethief.com or call +47 21 62 20 00 for reservations.

Opening Times: Open year-round.

5. Radisson Blu Royal Garden Hotel

Location: Trondheim, Norway

Located in the charming city of Trondheim, Radisson Blu Royal Garden Hotel is a top choice for those seeking comfort, modern amenities, and a central location. The hotel is ideally situated near the historic Nidaros Cathedral and the city's lively restaurants and shops. It is known for its high-end service and is a great base for exploring Trondheim's rich cultural heritage.

What's Special: The hotel offers a tranquil garden and a beautiful restaurant that focuses on locally sourced ingredients. The spacious rooms offer scenic views of the River Nidelva, making it an ideal spot for a peaceful getaway.

Price: Rooms start at approximately $200 per night.

How to Book: Book directly at www.radissonhotels.com or call +47 73 80 80 00.

Opening Times: Open year-round.

B. Budget-Friendly Options in Norway

Are you a solo traveler, a couple, or a family on a tight budget? Good news! There are plenty of affordable options that still provide an authentic Norwegian experience.

1. Citybox Oslo

Citybox

Citybox Oslo

Prinsens gate 6, 0152 Oslo, Norway — Directions

4.2 ★★★★

View larger map

SCAN THE QR CODE

1. Open your device camera app.
2. Position the QR code in the camera frame.
3. Hold your phone steady.
4. Wait for the code to be recognized.
5. Once recognized, tap on the notification or follow the prompt to access the content or action associated with the Qr code

Location: Oslo, Norway

Located in the heart of Oslo, Citybox Oslo is a modern, self-service hotel that offers great value for money. This budget-friendly gem is perfect for travelers who want to stay in the city center without spending a fortune. With its minimalist design and convenient amenities, it provides a comfortable and affordable base for exploring Oslo.

What's Special: The hotel offers 24/7 check-in via automated kiosks, making it incredibly convenient for those arriving at odd hours. Rooms are clean, simple, and functional, with everything you need for a short stay. It's a no-frills option that focuses on offering value without compromising on quality.

Price: Prices start at around $100 per night.

How to Book: Book directly through www.citybox.no or call +47 23 35 50 50 for more information.

Opening Times: Open year-round.

2. Anker Hostel

Anker Hostel

Anker Hostel

Storgata 53H, 0182 Oslo, Norway

Directions

3.8 ★★★★

View larger map

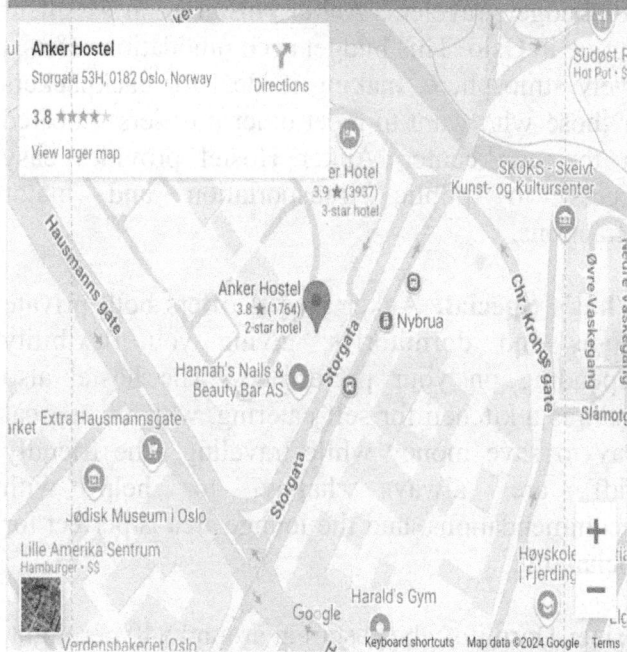

Anker Hostel
3.8 ★ (1764)
2-star hotel

SCAN THE QR CODE

1. Open your device camera app.
2. Position the QR code in the camera frame.
3. Hold your phone steady.
4. Wait for the code to be recognized.
5. Once recognized, tap on the notification or follow the prompt to access the content or action associated with the Qr code

Location: Oslo, Norway

For budget travelers, Anker Hostel is an excellent choice in Oslo. This budget accommodation offers a lively atmosphere, making it ideal for backpackers or those who want to meet other travelers. Located in the city center, Anker Hostel provides easy access to public transportation and major attractions.

What's Special: Anker Hostel offers both private rooms and dormitories, giving you flexibility depending on your preferences. The hostel also features a kitchen for self-catering, which is a great way to save money while traveling. The friendly staff are always happy to help with recommendations, and the lounge area is perfect for socializing.

Price: Dormitory beds start at around $40 per night, and private rooms begin at $80 per night.

How to Book: Visit www.ankerhostel.no or call +47 22 17 58 80 for bookings.

Opening Times: Open year-round.

3. Scandic Hotels

Scandic Hotels

Scandic Holmenkollen Park H...
Kongeveien 26, 0787 Oslo, Norway — Directions

4.3 ★★★★★

View larger map

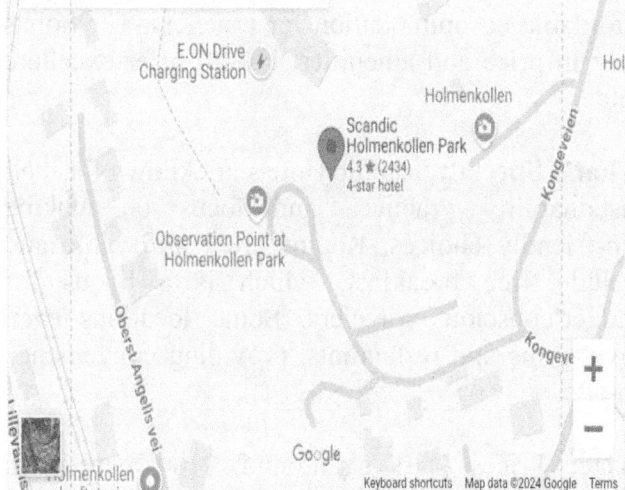

E.ON Drive
Charging Station

Holmenkollen

Scandic
Holmenkollen Park
4.3 ★ (2434)
4-star hotel

Observation Point at
Holmenkollen Park

Oberst Angells vei

Kongeveien

Google
Keyboard shortcuts   Map data ©2024 Google   Terms

SCAN THE QR CODE

1. Open your device camera app.
2. Position the QR code in the camera frame.
3. Hold your phone steady.
4. Wait for the code to be recognized.
5. Once recognized, tap on the notification or follow the prompt to access the content or action associated with the Qr code

Location: Various locations across Norway

If you're looking for a chain that offers consistent quality at a reasonable price, Scandic Hotels is a fantastic choice. With over 20 locations across Norway, including cities like Oslo, Bergen, and Trondheim, Scandic provides reliable and affordable accommodation for travelers. The hotels vary in price and amenities, but all offer excellent value.

What's Special: Scandic Hotels are known for their sustainability practices and focus on making eco-friendly choices. Rooms are comfortable and include free breakfast, which is a bonus for budget-conscious travelers. Some locations even have gyms and restaurants, providing convenience on-site.

Price: Prices start at around $100 per night, depending on the location and time of booking.

How to Book: You can book through [www.scandichotels.com](https://www.scandichotel s.com) or call the specific hotel location for details.

Opening Times: Open year-round.

4. Airbnb (Various Locations)

Location: Across Norway

For a more personalized experience, Airbnb is an excellent option for budget travelers looking for unique accommodations. Whether you're staying in a cozy apartment in Bergen, a charming cabin in the mountains, or a shared room in Oslo, Airbnb offers a wide range of budget-friendly choices across Norway.

What's Special: Airbnb provides a variety of options that cater to different budgets. You can rent entire homes, private rooms, or shared spaces, giving you flexibility and a more local experience. It's also a great way to meet Norwegians and get insider tips about the area. Prices vary widely, so it's easy to find something that fits your budget.

Price: Prices can range from $40 per night for shared rooms to $150+ for private apartments or homes.

How to Book: Visit www.airbnb.com and search for accommodations in the specific city or area you want to visit.

Opening Times: Open year-round.

5. Thon Hotel Spectrum

Thon Hotel Spectrum

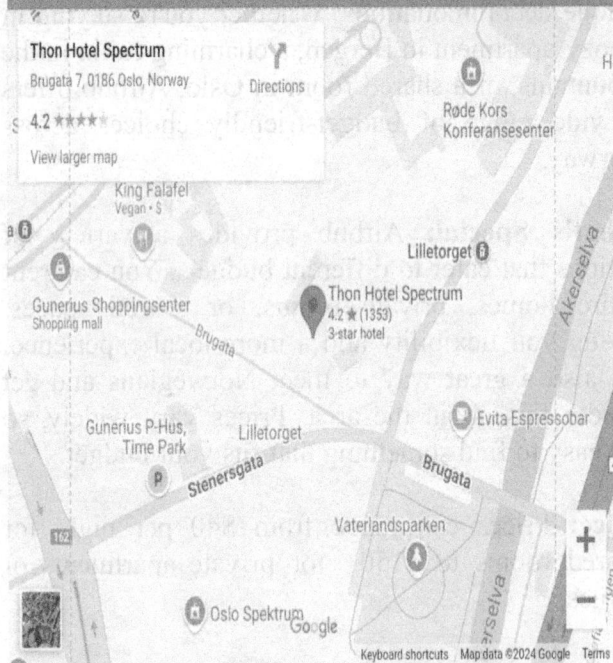

Thon Hotel Spectrum
Brugata 7, 0186 Oslo, Norway

Directions

4.2 ★★★★

View larger map

King Falafel
Vegan · $

Lilletorget

Gunerius Shoppingsenter
Shopping mall

Brugata

Thon Hotel Spectrum
4.2 ★ (1353)
3-star hotel

Røde Kors
Konferansesenter

Akerselva

Gunerius P-Hus,
Time Park

Lilletorget

Evita Espressobar

Stenersgata

Brugata

Vaterlandsparken

Oslo Spektrum Google

Keyboard shortcuts   Map data ©2024 Google   Terms

SCAN THE QR CODE

1. Open your device camera app.
2. Position the QR code in the camera frame.
3. Hold your phone steady.
4. Wait for the code to be recognized.
5. Once recognized, tap on the notification or follow the prompt to access the content or action associated with the Qr code

Location: Oslo, Norway

Located just a short walk from Oslo's central train station, Thon Hotel Spectrum offers affordable yet comfortable accommodation in the heart of the city. It's perfect for those who want to be close to all the major attractions and public transportation without spending too much on lodging.

What's Special: Thon Hotels are known for their excellent breakfast buffets, and the Spectrum location is no exception. The rooms are modern, clean, and comfortable, with all the amenities you need for a pleasant stay. The hotel also offers free Wi-Fi and a cozy lounge area.

Price: Prices start around $120 per night.

How to Book: Book through www.thonhotels.com or call +47 23 35 50 00 for reservations.

Opening Times: Open year-round.

Chapter 8: Outdoor Activities and Adventures

A. Best Hikes in Norway for Beginners and Experts

Let's explore some of the best hikes this beautiful country has to offer.

For Beginners

1. Rondane National Park: Rondvassbu to Peer Gynt Cabin

- **Why It's Great:** This gentle trail in Rondane National Park offers serene views of rolling hills and alpine lakes. It's perfect for first-timers or those looking for a relaxing hike.
- **Distance**: 6 km (~3.7 miles) round trip.
- **Good to Know:** The trail is well-marked and ends at the charming Peer Gynt Cabin, where you can enjoy a snack and a warm drink.

2. Storseterfossen Waterfall Hike (Geiranger)

- **Why It's Great:** This short hike takes you to a unique waterfall you can walk behind! It's a family-friendly adventure with stunning views of the Geirangerfjord along the way.
- **Distance**: 4.5 km (~2.8 miles) round trip.
- **Good to Know:** The trail is easy to follow and suitable for kids.

3. Prest Mountain (Aurland)

- **Why It's Great:** A moderate hike with a big reward—sweeping views of the Aurlandsfjord. It's a fantastic option for beginners ready to tackle a slightly steeper trail.
- **Distance**: 4 km (~2.5 miles) round trip.
- **Good to Know:** The trail is best in summer and fall when conditions are dry.

For Experts

1. Trolltunga (The Troll's Tongue)

- **Why It's Great:** This iconic hike leads to a dramatic cliff jutting out over Lake Ringedalsvatnet. The views are jaw-dropping, and the experience is unforgettable.
- **Distance:** 28 km (~17.4 miles) round trip.
- **Good to Know:** The hike is strenuous and takes 10–12 hours, so start early and come

prepared with proper gear and plenty of water.

2. Romsdalseggen Ridge (Åndalsnes)
- **Why It's Great:** Known as one of Norway's most beautiful hikes, this ridge offers panoramic views of the Romsdal Alps, fjords, and lush valleys. It's a challenging trail but worth every step.
- **Distance**: 10 km (~6.2 miles) one way.
- **Good to Know:** The trail requires good fitness levels and is best hiked in summer or early autumn.

3. Besseggen Ridge (Jotunheimen National Park)
- **Why It's Great:** This famous hike features breathtaking views of Gjende and Bessvatnet lakes, with one emerald green and the other deep blue. It's a bucket-list hike for adventure seekers.
- **Distance**: 14 km (~8.7 miles) one way.
- **Good to Know:** Most hikers take a boat to the trailhead and hike back, so plan your day accordingly.

Tips for a Great Hiking Experience

1. Check the Weather: Norway's weather can change quickly, so always check conditions before heading out.
2. Dress in Layers: Pack waterproof and windproof clothing, even in summer.

3. Bring Snacks and Water: Keep yourself fueled and hydrated during the hike.

4. Start Early: Many trails take several hours to complete, so give yourself plenty of daylight.

5. Follow Trail Markers: Norway's trails are well-marked, but always stick to the path to protect the environment and stay safe.

Best Time to Hike in Norway

- **Summer (June to August):** The most popular time for hiking, with long daylight hours and snow-free trails.
- **Autumn (September to October):** Trails are quieter, and the fall colors are spectacular.
- **Winter (November to March):** Some trails are accessible, but most require snowshoes or skis.
- **Spring (April to May):** Lower trails start to thaw, offering early-season hiking opportunities.

B. Kayaking, Fjord Cruises, and Water Adventures

Norway is a land of water—its fjords, rivers, and coastline offer some of the most breathtaking and serene experiences you can imagine. Let's dive in and explore the best ways to experience Norway from the water!

Kayaking

1. Nærøyfjord:
- **Why You'll Love It**: Paddling through this UNESCO World Heritage fjord feels like stepping into a postcard. The towering cliffs and cascading waterfalls create a peaceful, almost otherworldly setting.
- **Good to Know:** Kayak rentals and guided tours are available in the nearby village of Gudvangen.

2. Geirangerfjord:
- **Why You'll Love It:** Imagine paddling beneath the famous Seven Sisters Waterfall, with fjord cliffs rising dramatically on either side. It's a once-in-a-lifetime experience.
- **Good to Know:** Tours cater to beginners and experienced kayakers alike, making it accessible to everyone.

3. The Lofoten Islands: Arctic Magic
- **Why You'll Love It:** Paddle through crystal-clear Arctic waters, surrounded by jagged peaks and colorful fishing villages. Keep an eye out for sea eagles soaring overhead!
- **Good to Know:** Summer offers the Midnight Sun, while winter brings chances to kayak under the Northern Lights.

Fjord Cruises

1. Sognefjord:

- **Why You'll Love It:** As Norway's longest and deepest fjord, Sognefjord offers endless beauty. Cruises take you through its serene waters, surrounded by dramatic cliffs and charming villages.
- **What to Do:** Hop on a ferry from Flåm or Gudvangen for a scenic journey. Combine your cruise with the Flåm Railway for the ultimate fjord adventure.

2. **Hardangerfjord:**
- **Why You'll Love It:** Known for its fruit orchards and stunning waterfalls like Vøringsfossen, this fjord offers a mix of natural beauty and cultural charm.
- **What to Do:** Take a cider-tasting cruise to explore the local flavors while enjoying the scenery.

3. **Lysefjord:**
- **Why You'll Love It:** Home to the famous Pulpit Rock (Preikestolen) and Kjerag Boulder, Lysefjord is perfect for those who love adventure. Cruises offer stunning views of these landmarks from the water.
- **What to Do:** Combine your cruise with a hike for the ultimate fjord experience.

Other Water Adventures in Norway

1. **Whitewater Rafting**
- **Where**: Rivers like Sjoa in Gudbrandsdalen are perfect for rafting enthusiasts.

- **Why You'll Love It:** Experience the rush of navigating rapids while surrounded by Norway's lush landscapes.

2. Sea Fishing
- **Where**: Try fishing in the Arctic waters around the Lofoten Islands or the calmer fjords of Tromsø.
- **Why You'll Love It:** Norway's waters are teeming with cod, halibut, and mackerel, making it a paradise for anglers.

3. RIB Boat Adventures
- **Where**: Popular in Tromsø, Bergen, and the Lofoten Islands.
- **Why You'll Love It:** Zoom through fjords on a high-speed RIB boat, getting up close to cliffs, waterfalls, and even seals or porpoises.

Best Time for Water Adventures in Norway

- **Summer (June to August):** The best time for kayaking and fjord cruises, with long daylight hours and warm weather.
- **Autumn (September to October):** A quieter time with stunning fall colors reflected in the water.
- **Winter (November to March):** Unique Arctic experiences like kayaking under the Northern Lights or cruising through snow-covered fjords.

Tips for Enjoying Norway's Water Adventures

1. Dress for the Weather: Even in summer, fjord waters can be chilly. Wear layers and waterproof gear.

2. Book in Advance: Fjord cruises and guided kayak tours can fill up quickly, especially during peak season.

3. Bring a Camera: The views are spectacular, so make sure to capture the memories.

C. Skiing and Snowboarding in Norway's Alpine Resorts

Why Ski in Norway?

Norway's ski culture is legendary. This is the birthplace of skiing, and Norwegians have been gliding through the snow for centuries. The country's diverse landscapes mean you'll find everything from family-friendly resorts with gentle slopes to adrenaline-pumping runs and off-piste adventures. Add in cozy lodges, stunning fjord views, and a chance to see the Northern Lights, and you have a ski trip like no other.

Top Ski Resorts in Norway

1. Trysil:
- **Why It's Awesome:** With over 70 kilometers of slopes and excellent facilities for families, Trysil is Norway's largest and

most popular ski resort. Its well-groomed runs are perfect for beginners and intermediates, but advanced skiers will also find challenges.

- **What to Do:** Enjoy night skiing, snow parks, and après-ski activities at cozy mountain restaurants.
- **Good to Know:** Located 2.5 hours from Oslo, it's easily accessible by car or bus.

2. Hemsedal:
- **Why It's Awesome**: Known for its long ski season and varied terrain, Hemsedal offers everything from beginner-friendly runs to advanced slopes and off-piste areas. It's also home to excellent snow parks for freestyle enthusiasts.
- **What to Do:** Try cross-country skiing trails or relax at the vibrant après-ski scene.
- **Good to Know:** Hemsedal is about 3 hours from Oslo by car or bus.

3. Hafjell:
- **Why It's Awesome:** Located near Lillehammer, Hafjell is perfect for families and offers a great mix of beginner and intermediate slopes. It also has a dedicated kids' area and excellent snow parks.
- **What to Do:** Combine your skiing trip with a visit to the nearby Olympic venues from the 1994 Winter Games.

- **Good to Know:** Hafjell is just a 15-minute drive from Lillehammer, making it easy to reach.

4. **Narvik:**
   - **Why It's Awesome:** If you're looking for a unique experience, Narvik offers Arctic skiing with dramatic fjord views. The resort is known for its challenging slopes and backcountry opportunities.
   - **What to Do:** Ski under the Northern Lights or enjoy off-piste runs with a guide.
   - **Good to Know:** Narvik is accessible by train or a short flight from Oslo.

5. **Geilo:**
   - **Why It's Awesome**: One of Norway's oldest ski resorts, Geilo offers a mix of alpine skiing, cross-country trails, and snowboarding options. It's a charming resort with a cozy village feel.
   - **What to Do:** Try dog sledding, snowshoeing, or relax at one of Geilo's luxurious spas.
   - **Good to Know:** Located halfway between Oslo and Bergen, it's easy to reach by train.

Best Time to Ski in Norway

- **Winter (December to February):** The peak ski season with guaranteed snow and long nights perfect for cozying up by the fire.

- **Spring (March to April):** Longer daylight hours, sunny slopes, and great snow conditions make this a favorite time for skiing.
- **Autumn (October to November):** Early snowfall often allows for skiing in northern resorts.

What Makes Norway's Skiing Unique?

1. Northern Lights Skiing: In Arctic regions like Narvik, you might catch the Northern Lights while skiing at night—a truly magical experience.
2. Skiing to Fjords: Resorts like Stranda let you ski down mountains with stunning fjord views.
3. Cross-Country Trails: Norway's cross-country skiing network is unmatched, offering hundreds of kilometers of groomed trails for all skill levels.

Tips for Skiing in Norway

1. Dress Warmly: Norway's winters can be cold, so layer up with thermal clothing, waterproof outerwear, and insulated gloves.
2. Book Early: Resorts like Trysil and Hemsedal are popular, especially during school holidays, so secure your accommodation and lift passes in advance.
3. Take a Lesson: Most resorts offer English-speaking instructors, perfect for beginners or those looking to improve their technique.

4. **Try Something New:** Many resorts also offer unique activities like dog sledding, snowshoeing, and ice fishing.

D. Fishing and Wildlife Safaris

Let's dive into the best fishing spots and wildlife safaris that this majestic country has to offer!

Fishing in Norway

1. **Lofoten Islands:**
   - **Why It's Awesome:** The Lofoten Islands are legendary for their cod fishing, particularly during the winter season when Arctic cod migrate to the area.
   - **What to Do:** Join a fishing boat tour or cast your line from the shore. You might even catch your own dinner!
   - **Good to Know:** The islands are also famous for stockfish (dried cod), a local delicacy with centuries of history.

2. **Tromsø:**
   - **Why It's Awesome:** Tromsø offers excellent fishing opportunities, from catching halibut and cod to trying your hand at king crab fishing.
   - **What to Do:** Book a guided fishing tour to learn about traditional Norwegian techniques.

3. **Sognefjord:**

- **Why It's Awesome:** As Norway's longest fjord, Sognefjord offers plenty of opportunities for fishing while surrounded by breathtaking scenery.
- **What to Do:** Rent a boat or join a local guide to fish for trout, salmon, and mackerel.

4. **Rivers and Lakes:**
   - **Why It's Awesome:** Norway's rivers and lakes are ideal for catching salmon, trout, and Arctic char. Top spots include the Gaula River (famous for salmon) and Lake Mjøsa (Norway's largest lake).
   - **Good to Know:** Be sure to purchase a fishing license, required for freshwater fishing in Norway.

Wildlife Safaris

1. **Whale Watching in Tromsø and Vesterålen**
   - **Why It's Awesome:** Norway is one of the best places in the world for whale watching. Humpback whales, orcas, and even sperm whales migrate to the Arctic waters during winter.
   - **What to Do:** Join a guided whale safari to witness these majestic creatures up close. Winter is the best season for whale watching in northern Norway.

2. **Reindeer Safaris in Finnmark**

- **Why It's Awesome:** Experience the traditional Sami way of life by joining a reindeer sledding safari in Finnmark. This unique adventure takes you deep into Arctic culture and landscapes.
- **What to Do:** Learn about the Sami people, their herding traditions, and enjoy a cozy meal in a traditional lavvu (tent).

3. Musk Ox Safaris in Dovrefjell National Park
- **Why It's Awesome:** Step into Norway's wilderness to see musk oxen, ancient animals that roamed during the Ice Age. These powerful creatures can weigh up to 400 kilograms!
- **What to Do:** Guided safaris ensure a safe and thrilling experience, with expert guides leading you to the best viewing spots.

4. Bird Watching in Varanger Peninsula
- **Why It's Awesome:** The Varanger Peninsula is a paradise for bird enthusiasts, home to puffins, sea eagles, and Arctic birds like the snowy owl.
- **What to Do:** Explore nature reserves and coastal cliffs for the best sightings. Spring and summer are the best seasons for bird watching.

5. Polar Bear Safaris in Svalbard
- **Why It's Awesome:** Svalbard is one of the few places in the world where you can see polar bears in their natural habitat. While

sightings are not guaranteed, boat or snowmobile tours often bring you close to the Arctic wildlife, including seals and walruses.

- **Good to Know:** Polar bear safaris are tightly regulated to ensure safety and conservation.

Tips for Fishing and Wildlife Safaris

1. Dress for the Weather: Norway's climate can be unpredictable, especially in the Arctic. Layers and waterproof gear are essential.
2. Book in Advance: Guided tours and safaris often fill up quickly, especially during peak seasons.
3. Respect Nature: Follow all rules and guidelines to protect Norway's wildlife and pristine environment.
4. Bring Binoculars and Cameras: Wildlife encounters are unforgettable, so make sure you're ready to capture the moment.

Best Time for Fishing and Safaris in Norway

Fishing:
- **Winter (January to March):** Best for cod fishing in the Lofoten Islands.
- **Summer (June to August):** Prime time for salmon and freshwater fishing.

Wildlife Safaris:
- **Winter (November to March):** Ideal for whale watching, reindeer safaris, and polar bear sightings.

- **Spring and Summer (May to August):** Great for bird watching, musk ox safaris, and fjord adventures.

E. Adventure Sports

Norway isn't just about serene fjords and picturesque villages—it's also an adrenaline junkie's paradise! Let's dive into some of the most thrilling outdoor activities that this country has to offer.

Whitewater Rafting

1. Sjoa River:
- **Why It's Awesome:** Known as the best whitewater rafting destination in Norway, the Sjoa River offers a range of rapids, from beginner-friendly waves to wild, challenging runs for seasoned adventurers.
- **What to Do:** Book a guided rafting tour to experience the thrill of paddling through rapids surrounded by stunning Norwegian scenery.
- **Good to Know:** Tours are available from May to September, with half-day and full-day options.

2. Numedalslågen River
- **Why It's Awesome:** This river near Geilo combines exciting rapids with stretches of

calm water, allowing you to soak in the surrounding beauty.

- **What to Do:** Choose a tour that matches your skill level, or try family-friendly rafting trips.

3. Voss:

Why It's Awesome: Voss is a hub for outdoor sports, and its rivers offer rafting adventures for all experience levels. It's also home to the annual Extreme Sports Week in June, which attracts thrill-seekers from around the world.

- **Good to Know:** After rafting, explore other activities in the area, like kayaking or zip-lining.

Ice Climbing

1. Rjukan:

- **Why It's Awesome:** With over 150 frozen waterfalls, Rjukan is Norway's top destination for ice climbing. Whether you're a beginner or a pro, there's a route for you.
- **What to Do:** Join a guided ice climbing session to learn the basics or tackle more challenging routes with experienced instructors.
- **Good to Know:** The ice climbing season typically runs from December to March.

2. Lyngen Alps:

- **Why It's Awesome:** The Lyngen Alps in northern Norway offer ice climbing experiences with a side of Arctic beauty. Imagine scaling icy cliffs while gazing out at snow-covered fjords.

- **What to Do:** Combine ice climbing with other Arctic adventures, like skiing or Northern Lights hunting.

3. Hemsedal:

- **Why It's Awesome:** Hemsedal's frozen waterfalls provide a variety of routes for ice climbers, from easy ascents to technical climbs. It's perfect for those looking to test their limits.

Paragliding

1. Voss:

- **Why It's Awesome:** Voss is not only a rafting hotspot but also one of the best places for paragliding in Norway. Launch from the mountains and glide over valleys, fjords, and rivers—it's a view you'll never forget.
- **Good to Know:** Tandem flights are available for beginners, so no prior experience is needed.

2. Gudvangen:

- **Why It's Awesome:** Paragliding in Gudvangen offers stunning aerial views of the Nærøyfjord, a UNESCO World Heritage site. It's a serene yet thrilling way to experience Norway's fjord landscapes.

3. Loen:
- **Why It's Awesome**: Take off from the mountains near Loen and soar above the turquoise waters of the Nordfjord and the mighty Jostedalsbreen Glacier. It's an unforgettable Arctic adventure.

Best Time for Adventure Sports in Norway

- **Summer (June to August):** Perfect for rafting and paragliding, with long daylight hours and warmer temperatures.
- **Winter (December to March):** Ideal for ice climbing and winter paragliding, especially in Arctic regions.

Tips for Adventurers

1. Gear Up: Most tours provide equipment, but wear weather-appropriate clothing and sturdy shoes.
2. Follow the Experts: Guided tours and professional instructors ensure safety and maximize your experience.
3. Capture the Moment: Bring a waterproof camera or GoPro to document your adventure.

Chapter 9: Exploring Norway's Rich Culture

A. Best Restaurants in Norway

Here are some of the best restaurants across the country that you should consider for a memorable dining experience.

1. Maaemo (Oslo)

Location: Oslo, Norway

If you're looking for an unforgettable fine-dining experience in Norway, Maaemo in Oslo is a must. This Michelin-starred restaurant is renowned for its creative, modern take on Nordic cuisine. Maaemo's approach is all about locally sourced ingredients and seasonal flavors, with a focus on sustainability and the environment.

- **What's Special:** Maaemo is a sensory journey that emphasizes the purity of nature's bounty. Each dish is an artistic creation, using ingredients that are foraged, farmed, or caught from the pristine landscapes of Norway. The tasting menu changes seasonally, offering a unique experience every time you visit.

- **Price:** Tasting menus start around $300 per person.

- **How to Book:** Reservations are essential. Book online through www.maaemo.no.

- **Opening Times:** Tuesday to Saturday, 5:30 PM – 11:00 PM.

2. <u>Re-naa</u> (Stavanger)

Location: Stavanger, Norway

Located in the heart of Stavanger, Re-naa is a Michelin-starred restaurant known for its exceptional Nordic cuisine with a modern twist. Chef Roger Asakil Joya takes inspiration from the region's natural bounty, offering inventive dishes that showcase the best of local ingredients.

- **What's Special:** Re-naa has an intimate atmosphere, with a personalized approach to dining. The restaurant offers a tasting menu that changes frequently, with wine pairings carefully selected to complement each dish. It's a place for food enthusiasts who want to explore the depth of Norwegian flavors with a sophisticated, contemporary touch.

- **Price:** Tasting menu starts at around $200 per person.

- **How to Book:** Book online at www.renaa.no or call +47 51 52 30 00.

- **Opening Times:** Wednesday to Saturday, 5:00 PM – 10:00 PM.

3. Lofoten Fiskerestaurant (Oslo)

Location: Oslo, Norway

If you're in Oslo and craving fresh seafood, Lofoten Fiskerestaurant is the place to go. Located by the Oslo fjord, this restaurant specializes in traditional Norwegian seafood dishes, featuring the freshest fish, shellfish, and locally caught delicacies.

- **What's Special:** The restaurant offers a variety of classic seafood dishes such as Røkt Laks (smoked salmon), Skrei (Norwegian cod), and Kreps (Norwegian crayfish). Enjoying your meal with a view of the harbor adds to the charm of this charming seafood spot.

- **Price:** A meal for two with wine can cost around $100-$150.

- **How to Book:** Reservations can be made through www.lofoten.no or by calling +47 22 83 15 80.

- **Opening Times:** Daily, 11:00 AM – 11:00 PM.

4. Mathallen Oslo (Oslo)

Location: Oslo, Norway

For a more casual yet vibrant dining experience, Mathallen Oslo is a food market that offers a wide variety of Norwegian and international cuisines. Situated in the Vulkan area, this indoor market has over 30 food stalls and restaurants, each offering a unique dish made with local and organic ingredients.

- **What's Special**: From Norwegian cheese and cured meats to artisanal breads and fresh seafood, Mathallen provides a true taste of Norwegian food culture. It's also a great place to sample international flavors, with everything from Italian pizza to Asian street food.

- **Price:** The prices vary depending on the vendor, but a meal can range from $15 to $50.

- **How to Book:** No reservations required, but you can check the [Mathallen Oslo website](https://www.mathallen.no) for more details.

- **Opening Times:** Monday to Friday, 10:00 AM – 8:00 PM; Saturday, 10:00 AM – 6:00 PM; Sunday, Closed.

5. Fjord Restaurant (Oslo)

Location: Oslo, Norway

As the name suggests, Fjord Restaurant specializes in seafood, particularly focusing on the finest fish and shellfish from Norwegian waters. With a modern and chic ambiance, this is a place where you can enjoy an elegant yet relaxed meal that showcases the purity of Norwegian seafood.

- **What's Special:** Fjord's menu changes frequently, but it always highlights the freshest catches of the day. The dishes are artfully presented, and the wine list is curated to complement the flavors of the ocean. The restaurant's minimalist yet stylish design adds to the experience.

- **Price:** Main courses range from $30 to $60, with tasting menus available for $120 per person.

- **How to Book:** Visit www.fjordrestaurant.no or call +47 22 83 81 00.

- **Opening Times:** Monday to Saturday, 5:30 PM – 10:00 PM.

6. Credo (Trondheim)

Location: Trondheim, Norway

A Michelin-starred restaurant in Trondheim, Credo is dedicated to sustainable and locally sourced food. Chef Heidi Bjerkan and her team focus on creating dishes that are deeply connected to Norwegian nature, with a menu that changes with the seasons.

- **What's Special:** Credo's tasting menu is designed around the best local ingredients and reflects the rich culinary traditions of the Trøndelag region. The restaurant emphasizes a farm-to-table approach, using organic produce and sustainable farming practices.

- **Price:** Tasting menu starts around $150 per person.

- **How to Book:** Book through www.credorestaurant.no or call +47 73 50 92 00.

- **Opening Times:** Wednesday to Saturday, 5:00 PM – 10:00 PM.

7. Solsiden Restaurant (Trondheim)

- **Location:** Trondheim, Norway

For a more relaxed yet flavorful dining experience in Trondheim, Solsiden Restaurant offers a stunning waterfront setting with a focus on fresh seafood. Whether you're looking to enjoy a casual lunch or an elegant dinner, Solsiden offers the perfect atmosphere.

- **What's Special:** Specializing in seafood, the restaurant features dishes made with ingredients sourced from Norway's vast coastline. The menu includes both traditional Norwegian favorites and modern interpretations, with options for both meat lovers and vegetarians.

- **Price:** Main courses range from $20 to $50.

- **How to Book:** Call +47 73 89 60 70 or check their website at www.solsidenrestaurant.no.

- **Opening Times:** Daily, 11:00 AM – 10:00 PM.

B. Traditional Norwegian Cuisine

Let's explore some of the most iconic dishes and culinary experiences Norway has to offer!

Breakfast:

1. Brown Cheese (Brunost)
  - **Why It's Iconic:** This sweet, caramel-like cheese is a staple on Norwegian breakfast tables. Often served on toast or crispbread, brunost has a flavor that's uniquely Norwegian.
  - **Good to Know:** Try it with a dollop of jam for the perfect balance of sweet and savory.

2. Knekkebrød (Crispbread)
  - **Why It's Iconic:** These crunchy, versatile crackers are topped with everything from cheese and cured meats to butter and jam. They're healthy, filling, and oh-so-Norwegian.

3. Smoked Salmon
  - **Why It's Iconic:** Norway is famous for its salmon, and a breakfast plate with smoked salmon, dill, and lemon is the perfect way to start your day.

Lunch:

1. Open-Faced Sandwiches (Smørbrød)
- **Why It's Iconic:** These sandwiches are as beautiful as they are delicious. Topped with smoked fish, boiled eggs, or shrimp, they're a popular lunch option.
- **Good to Know:** Norwegians often pair their smørbrød with a strong cup of black coffee.

2. Rømmegrøt (Sour Cream Porridge)
- **Why It's Iconic:** A traditional dish often enjoyed during celebrations, rømmegrøt is creamy and comforting, served with sugar, cinnamon, and butter.

Dinner:

1. Fårikål (Lamb and Cabbage Stew)
- **Why It's Iconic:** Named Norway's national dish, fårikål is a hearty stew made with lamb, cabbage, and whole black peppercorns. It's simple yet deeply satisfying.
- **Good to Know:** Best enjoyed in autumn, during the lambing season.

2. Klippfisk (Dried and Salted Cod)
- **Why It's Iconic:** This preserved fish has been a staple in Norwegian cuisine for centuries. Often baked or fried, it's typically served with potatoes and vegetables.

3. Reindeer Meat

- **Why It's Iconic:** A specialty in northern Norway, reindeer is tender, lean, and often served as a steak or in stews. Pair it with lingonberries for a traditional Arctic flavor.

Desserts:

1. Krumkake
- **Why It's Iconic:** These delicate, cone-shaped cookies are filled with whipped cream and often served during Christmas.
- **Good to Know:** They're made using a special decorative iron, which gives them their intricate patterns.

2. Cloudberries with Cream (Multekrem)
- **Why It's Iconic:** These rare Arctic berries are a treasured ingredient in Norwegian desserts. Paired with whipped cream, they're a sweet and tangy treat.

3. Skillingsboller (Cinnamon Buns)
- **Why It's Iconic:** Found in bakeries across Norway, these buns are soft, sweet, and filled with cinnamon goodness. They're perfect with a cup of coffee.

Drinks:

1. Aquavit
- **Why It's Iconic:** This spiced spirit, distilled from potatoes or grain, is Norway's

traditional drink. It's often enjoyed during festive meals or as a warming toast.

2. Local Ciders and Beers
- **Why It's Iconic:** Norway's craft cider and beer scene is thriving, with flavors inspired by local fruits, herbs, and traditions.

3. Kaffe (Coffee)
- **Why It's Iconic:** Norwegians take their coffee seriously. Whether it's a morning brew or an afternoon fika (coffee break), coffee is a big part of Norwegian culture.

Seasonal Delicacies

1. Rakfisk (Fermented Fish)
- **Why It's Iconic:** This strong-smelling delicacy is a winter tradition, served thinly sliced with potatoes, sour cream, and onions. It's an acquired taste but beloved by locals.

2. Lutefisk
- **Why It's Iconic**: This dish, made from dried cod rehydrated in lye, is a staple during Christmas. Served with bacon, peas, and mustard, it's a festive favorite.

C. Cultural Festivals and Events in 2025

Norway is a country that knows how to celebrate. From lively music festivals to ancient traditions, the calendar is packed with events that bring the country's rich culture to life. Let's explore some of the most exciting cultural events happening this year!

1. Bergen International Festival (Festspillene i Bergen)

- **When**: May 22 - June 5, 2025
- **Where**: Bergen
- **Why You'll Love It**: As one of the largest and most prestigious art festivals in Norway, this event showcases world-class performances in music, theater, opera, and dance. The charming city of Bergen becomes a hub of creativity and excitement, with venues ranging from historic halls to outdoor spaces.
- **What to Do:** Attend a symphony concert in Grieghallen or watch contemporary dance performances in the city's parks.

2. Midnight Sun Marathon

- **When**: June 21, 2025
- **Where**: Tromsø
- **Why You'll Love It:** Running a marathon at midnight under the golden glow of the Midnight Sun is a bucket-list experience. Whether you're participating or cheering from the sidelines, the energy of this event is infectious.

- **What to Do:** Explore Tromsø's vibrant nightlife after the race, or enjoy local Arctic cuisine at one of the city's restaurants.

3. Viking Festival in Avaldsnes
- **When**: June 6-9, 2025
- **Where**: Avaldsnes, near Haugesund
- **Why You'll Love It:** Step back in time and experience life as it was during the Viking Age. This family-friendly festival features Viking reenactments, crafts, music, and storytelling, all in the historic setting of Avaldsnes, Norway's oldest royal seat.
- **What to Do:** Watch thrilling Viking battles, try your hand at archery, or enjoy traditional Viking-style food.

4. Riddu Riđđu Festival
- **When**: July 10-14, 2025
- **Where:** Kåfjord, Northern Norway
- **Why You'll Love It:** This Indigenous music and culture festival celebrates the traditions of the Sami people and other Indigenous groups worldwide. With concerts, workshops, and art exhibitions, it's a vibrant and inclusive event.
- **What to Do:** Attend a joik (Sami singing) workshop, enjoy Sami cuisine, and learn about reindeer herding culture.

5. Oslo Jazz Festival
- **When:** August 11-16, 2025
- **Where**: Oslo

- **Why You'll Love It:** For jazz lovers, this festival is a must. Featuring performances by top international and Norwegian jazz artists, the festival takes place across multiple venues, including intimate clubs and grand concert halls.
- **What to Do:** Enjoy a riverside concert at the Mathallen food hall or discover up-and-coming artists in cozy venues around the city.

6. Arctic Light Festival
- **When**: January 31 - February 2, 2025
- **Where:** Harstad, Northern Norway
- **Why You'll Love It**: This festival celebrates the return of daylight after the polar night in northern Norway. It features music, light art installations, and local delicacies, all under the stunning Arctic skies.
- **What to Do:** Take part in a light-themed walking tour or enjoy concerts under the vibrant auroras.

7. Christmas Markets and Festivals
- **When**: November-December 2025
- **Where:** Nationwide (Oslo, Bergen, Trondheim, and more)
- **Why You'll Love It:** Norway transforms into a winter wonderland during the holiday season, with charming Christmas markets offering handmade gifts, festive treats, and warm mulled wine.

- **What to Do:** Visit Oslo's Spikersuppa Christmas Market for ice skating and local crafts or head to Bergen's market set against the scenic backdrop of the Bryggen Wharf.

Tips for Enjoying Norway's Festivals

1. Plan Ahead: Some events, like the Midnight Sun Marathon and Bergen International Festival, require tickets or registration. Book early to secure your spot.
2. Dress Appropriately: Norway's weather can be unpredictable, so wear layers and comfortable shoes.
3. Embrace the Local Vibes: Many festivals offer chances to try local food, music, and traditions—don't miss out!

D. Norway's Viking History and Heritage Sites

Step into the world of fierce warriors, skilled navigators, and legendary explorers—welcome to Norway's Viking heritage. The Vikings shaped the history and culture of Norway, leaving behind a legacy of fascinating stories, impressive ships, and ancient artifacts. If you're intrigued by this iconic era, Norway's Viking sites are the perfect places to dive into history. Let's explore the key destinations where the Viking spirit comes alive!

A Glimpse into Viking History

The Viking Age (approximately 800–1050 AD) was a time of exploration, trade, and conquest. Norwegian Vikings ventured far and wide, from the British Isles to Greenland, and even North America. They were master shipbuilders and navigators, known for their longships and advanced sailing techniques. While often portrayed as fierce raiders, Vikings were also traders, settlers, and farmers, contributing to the cultural and economic development of Europe.

Top Viking Heritage Sites in Norway

1. Viking Ship Museum (Oslo)

- **Why It's Iconic:** Home to the world's best-preserved Viking ships, including the famous Oseberg and Gokstad ships, this museum offers a window into Viking life and craftsmanship. These ships were used for both exploration and burial rituals, showcasing the importance of seafaring in Viking culture.
- **What to Do:** Marvel at the intricate carvings on the ships, explore the artifacts, and watch the short film Vikings Alive, which brings their voyages to life.
- **Good to Know**: The museum is part of the Museum of Cultural History, so your ticket grants access to other historical exhibitions.

2. Avaldsnes Viking Village (Haugesund)

- **Why It's Iconic**: Known as Norway's oldest royal seat, Avaldsnes was once a Viking power center. The reconstructed Viking village offers a glimpse into daily life during the Viking Age.

- **What to Do:** Visit St. Olav's Church, explore the Viking houses, and attend the annual Viking Festival in June.
- **Good to Know:** Guided tours bring the history of King Harald Fairhair, Norway's first king, to life.

3. Lofotr Viking Museum (Borg, Lofoten Islands)
- **Why It's Iconic:** Located on the site of the largest Viking longhouse ever discovered, this living history museum recreates the grandeur of Viking life in the Arctic.
- **What to Do**: Step inside the reconstructed longhouse, try traditional Viking games, and sail a replica Viking ship on the nearby fjord.
- **Good to Know:** The museum hosts interactive events like Viking feasts, where you can dine like a chieftain.

4. Gokstad Mound (Sandefjord)
- **Why It's Iconic:** This burial mound, where the Gokstad ship was discovered, is a significant archaeological site that sheds light on Viking burial customs.
- **What to Do:** Explore the mound and learn about the Viking chief buried here with a wealth of grave goods.

5. Kaupang Viking Town (Larvik)

- **Why It's Iconic**: Kaupang was one of Norway's first towns and a bustling Viking trading hub. Archaeological excavations have uncovered remains of houses, workshops, and trading goods.
- **What to Do**: Join a guided tour to see the excavation site and learn about Viking trade routes and craftsmanship.

Modern Connections to Viking Culture

Norway's Viking heritage isn't just about history—it's also celebrated in modern culture. From Viking-inspired festivals to replica longships sailing the seas, you'll find plenty of ways to connect with this fascinating era.

- **Festivals:** Events like the Viking Festival in Avaldsnes or the Midgard Viking Festival in Borre bring Viking history to life with reenactments, crafts, and storytelling.
- **TV and Film:** Shows like Vikings and Norsemen have sparked global interest in Viking history, with many filming locations in Norway.
- **Crafts and Cuisine**: Explore traditional Viking crafts at heritage sites or try Viking-inspired dishes like lamb stew or flatbread.

Tips for Exploring Viking Heritage

1. Plan Your Visits: Some museums and villages offer seasonal events, so check schedules in advance.

2. Engage with Guides: Guided tours and reenactments add depth to your experience, helping you visualize Viking life.

3. Try Interactive Activities: Sailing a Viking ship or participating in a feast makes the history come alive.

E. Museums, Art Galleries, and Theaters

Let's dive into some of the top cultural destinations that will captivate your imagination and enrich your journey.

Must-Visit Museums in Norway

1. The National Museum (Oslo)
- **Why It's Iconic:** This newly opened museum is the largest in the Nordic region, showcasing a vast collection of art, architecture, and design. The highlight? Edvard Munch's iconic painting, The Scream.
- **What to Do:** Explore the light-filled halls housing everything from ancient artifacts to modern masterpieces. Don't miss the rooftop terrace for stunning city views.

2. Munch Museum (Oslo)
- **Why It's Iconic:** Dedicated entirely to the works of Edvard Munch, this state-of-the-art

museum celebrates one of Norway's greatest artists.

- **What to Do:** Discover famous works like Madonna and The Scream alongside lesser-known pieces that delve into Munch's complex psyche.

3. **Fram Museum** (Oslo)
- **Why It's Iconic:** Dive into Norway's history of Arctic exploration. The Fram Museum houses the original Fram ship, used by legendary explorers like Roald Amundsen.
- **What to Do**: Step aboard the ship, explore interactive exhibits, and learn about Norway's polar expeditions.

4. **Bryggen Museum** (Bergen)
- **Why It's Iconic:** Located in the UNESCO World Heritage Bryggen Wharf area, this museum uncovers the city's rich trading history during the Hanseatic period.
- **What to Do:** Walk through reconstructed medieval structures and explore artifacts that reveal Bergen's maritime heritage.

5. **The Norwegian Petroleum Museum (Stavanger)**
- **Why It's Iconic:** This modern museum offers a fascinating look at Norway's oil and gas industry, which has shaped the nation's economy.

- **What to Do:** Enjoy interactive exhibits, from simulated oil platforms to hands-on activities for kids.

Art Galleries to Inspire You

1. Astrup Fearnley Museum of Modern Art (Oslo)
- **Why It's Iconic:** Located on the Oslo waterfront, this striking museum showcases contemporary works by international and Norwegian artists.
- **What to Do:** Wander through the galleries, admire works by Damien Hirst and Jeff Koons, and enjoy the stunning architecture of the building itself.

2. KODE Art Museums and Composer Homes (Bergen)
- **Why It's Iconic:** KODE is a collection of four art museums and the homes of famous composers like Edvard Grieg. It houses an impressive collection of Norwegian and international art.
- **What to Do:** Explore works by Edvard Munch and Nikolai Astrup, then visit Troldhaugen, Grieg's idyllic home.

3. Nordnorsk Kunstmuseum (Tromsø)
- **Why It's Iconic:** This museum highlights the unique culture and art of northern Norway, with a focus on Sami art and Arctic landscapes.

- **What to Do:** Discover traditional and modern pieces that celebrate the region's identity.

Theater and Performing Arts

1. National Theater (Oslo)
- **Why It's Iconic**: One of the oldest and most prestigious theaters in Norway, it hosts a variety of performances, from classic plays to contemporary productions.
- **What to Do:** Catch a performance during the annual Ibsen Festival, which celebrates Norway's most famous playwright, Henrik Ibsen.

2. Den Norske Opera & Ballett (Oslo Opera House)
- **Why It's Iconic**: This architectural masterpiece is a must-visit for its stunning design and world-class opera and ballet performances.
- **What to Do:** Take a guided tour, attend a show, or simply walk on the sloping roof for panoramic views of the Oslofjord.

3. The Arctic Philharmonic (Tromsø and Bodø)
- **Why It's Iconic**: The world's northernmost orchestra offers an unforgettable cultural experience with performances inspired by the Arctic environment.

- **What to Do:** Attend a concert that blends classical music with contemporary Arctic themes.

Cultural Tips for Visitors

1. Book Ahead: Popular museums and performances often sell out, so reserve your tickets in advance.
2. Take Your Time: Many museums and galleries offer more than meets the eye, so plan for a leisurely visit.
3. Embrace the Local Scene: Norway's smaller towns also have unique cultural centers worth exploring—don't limit yourself to the big cities.

Chapter 10: Travel Tips for Families and Groups

A. Norway with Kids

If you've got little explorers in tow, Norway is a dream destination. With its endless outdoor beauty, rich history, and family-friendly activities, this country makes it easy for families to bond while discovering new and exciting places together. Here's a guide to the best activities for families with kids of all ages in Norway.

1. Hiking with Kids: Nature's Playground

Norway's natural beauty is the ultimate outdoor playground for families. While some trails are more suited for experienced hikers, there are plenty of easy, family-friendly hikes that will leave everyone in awe of the country's dramatic landscapes.

- **Easy Trails for Young Kids:** The Rondane National Park offers gentle trails through picturesque valleys, where kids can enjoy the fresh air and spot local wildlife, such as reindeer and birds. The Himmelblå trail in Trollheimen is another easy hike that takes you past bubbling streams and open meadows—perfect for curious little adventurers.

- **Hiking to Iconic Spots:** For families with older children, consider tackling some of Norway's more famous hikes like Preikestolen (Pulpit Rock) or Kjeragbolten. These hikes offer spectacular views of the fjords and provide an exciting challenge for young teens and older kids, all while surrounded by breathtaking scenery.

2. Family-Friendly Wildlife Experiences

Norway is teeming with wildlife, and your kids will love getting the chance to see animals in their natural habitat. From the far north to the southern shores, these wildlife experiences are sure to delight.

- **Polar Bears and Reindeer at Polar Park:** Located in Bardu near the Arctic Circle, Polar Park is the world's northernmost animal park. It's a fantastic place for kids to learn about Arctic wildlife. They can see polar bears, wolves, lynx, and reindeer, all in the wildest setting you can imagine. Many tours offer an up-close look at these majestic creatures, making it a memorable experience for the entire family.

- **Whale Watching in Tromsø:** Tromsø, often referred to as the gateway to the Arctic, is an ideal location for whale watching, especially between October and January. Kids will be thrilled by the sight of humpback whales and orcas gliding through the frigid waters. Many family-friendly tours ensure a safe and educational experience with fun facts and interactive opportunities for young learners.

3. Viking Adventures for Kids

Norway's Viking past is fascinating, and it's one of the most captivating ways for kids to learn about history. With interactive museums, reenactments, and even living history villages, there's no shortage of ways to immerse your kids in the world of the Vikings.

- **Viking Ship Museum in Oslo:** The Viking Ship Museum is perfect for kids who want to see real Viking ships up close. They can also participate in fun activities like dressing up in Viking attire and learning how to row a Viking ship. The museum's exhibits are designed to be engaging for young audiences, making history come alive.

- **Lofotr Viking Museum:** On the Lofoten Islands, the Lofotr Viking Museum offers a hands-on experience where kids can try their hand at ancient Viking crafts, see replicas of Viking longhouses, and learn about daily life during the Viking Age. There are even opportunities for children to participate in archery or axe throwing, so they can step into the shoes of a Viking warrior.

4. Indoor Fun for Rainy Days

While Norway's natural wonders are breathtaking, the weather can be unpredictable. But don't let a little rain spoil the fun—Norway has a wide variety of indoor attractions that will keep your kids entertained for hours.

- **TusenFryd Amusement Park (Oslo):** Located just outside Oslo, TusenFryd is Norway's largest amusement park and is perfect for families with kids of all ages. With roller coasters, water rides, and kid-friendly attractions, it's the place to let your little ones burn off some energy. There's also a dedicated play area for younger kids, so everyone can have fun.

- **Norwegian Museum of Science and Technology (Oslo):** For a fun and educational experience, head to the Norwegian Museum of Science and Technology. With interactive exhibits on everything from space travel to robotics, this museum sparks curiosity and encourages hands-on learning. Kids will love experimenting with the exhibits and exploring the many activities designed just for them.

5. Enjoying Norway's Fairy-Tale Castles and Palaces

No family trip to Norway would be complete without exploring one of the country's beautiful castles. Kids will love the fairy-tale atmosphere of Norway's historic palaces and the chance to feel like royalty for a day.

- **Akershus Fortress (Oslo):** Located in Oslo, Akershus Fortress is a castle that dates back to the 1300s. Kids will enjoy exploring its towers and ramparts, imagining what life would have been like during medieval times. The fortress also offers stunning views of the Oslo Fjord, making it a great spot for family photos.

- **Kongsvinger Fortress:** Another fantastic castle to visit is Kongsvinger Fortress, located in the town of Kongsvinger. It's surrounded by lush green landscapes and offers guided tours where kids can learn about the fortress's military history and the important role it played during World War II.

6. The Magic of the Northern Lights and Midnight Sun

For families visiting Norway during the right time of year, experiencing the Northern Lights or the Midnight Sun is a once-in-a-lifetime experience. These incredible natural phenomena are sure to captivate both young and old.

- **Northern Lights in Tromsø:** Between September and March, Tromsø offers one of the best spots in the world to see the Northern Lights. Family-friendly Northern Lights tours are available, where kids can learn about the science behind this dazzling display while staying cozy in warm cabins, sipping hot chocolate. The lights are mesmerizing, and it's an experience that kids will remember forever.

- **Midnight Sun in the Lofoten Islands:** For something completely different, consider visiting the Lofoten Islands during the summer months when the sun never sets. The Midnight Sun creates a magical atmosphere, and kids will love the chance to stay up late without it getting dark. You can enjoy late-night picnics, hikes, or simply marvel at the unusual sunlight that makes the landscape glow.

7. Family-Friendly Accommodations in Norway

Finding family-friendly accommodations in Norway is easy, with a variety of options to suit every type of traveler. Whether you prefer a cozy cabin in the mountains or a hotel in the heart of a city, Norway has something for your family.

- **Scandic Hotels:** Scandic offers family-friendly hotels in cities like Oslo and Bergen. Many of these hotels have special family rooms, play areas, and kid-friendly menus, making them a great choice for parents traveling with children.
- **Cabins and Holiday Homes:** For a more unique experience, consider renting a cabin or hytte (holiday home) in Norway's countryside. These self-catering accommodations give families the flexibility to cook their own meals and enjoy a more relaxed, homely environment. Many cabins are located near outdoor attractions, making it easy to step outside and enjoy Norway's natural beauty.

B. Group Travel

Organizing a group trip to Norway is a thrilling adventure, but it also involves a fair amount of planning and budgeting. Let's break it down so you can plan an unforgettable trip while keeping your budget in check.

1. Choosing the Right Group Size and Type of Trip

The size of your group plays a crucial role in shaping your travel costs. Larger groups often benefit from group discounts, while smaller groups may have more flexibility but face higher individual costs.

- **Small Groups (2-8 people):** Traveling with a smaller group offers more flexibility when it comes to choosing activities and accommodations. However, you might miss out on group discounts for things like transportation or tours. For small groups, look for private cabins, boutique hotels, or tailored tours, but keep in mind that these options may come at a premium.

- **Medium Groups (9-20 people):** With a medium-sized group, you're more likely to access discounts for group tours, activities, and even accommodation. For example, you can rent larger holiday homes or book hotels that offer group rates. Although your costs may rise slightly compared to smaller groups, the savings on organized tours and transport can help offset the expenses.

- **Large Groups (20+ people):** Larger groups tend to benefit the most from cost savings, especially when it comes to transportation and tours. Bus rentals, group train tickets, and shared accommodation options such as dorms or larger holiday homes can significantly reduce per-person costs. The key here is to book early and ensure that you're taking full advantage of any group pricing discounts available.

2. Travel Seasons and Timing

The timing of your trip will have a major impact on the overall cost. If you're flexible with your travel dates, you can save a significant amount by avoiding Norway's peak tourist seasons.

- **Peak Season (June-August):** This is when most tourists flock to Norway, meaning higher prices for accommodation, tours, and flights. While the weather is at its best during summer, costs are typically the highest. If you plan to travel during this period, consider booking well in advance to lock in the best rates.

- **Off-Peak Seasons (Fall and Spring):** If you're aiming to save money, fall (September-November) and spring (March-May) are the best times to visit. Accommodation rates are lower, and you'll avoid the summer crowds. Activities like hiking, sightseeing, and visiting museums remain just as enjoyable, but the cost savings will be substantial.

- **Winter (December-February):** Winter in Norway can be expensive if you're planning on skiing or taking part in winter activities, but it can also be a great way to experience Norway's magical winter landscapes. If you're open to more affordable winter activities like exploring the Northern Lights or snowshoeing, winter can be a more budget-friendly time to visit compared to peak summer.

3. Accommodation and Group Rates

Accommodation is one of the largest expenses when traveling with a group. The good news is that Norway offers a wide range of accommodation options that cater to groups, from hotels to private cabins and hostels.

- **Private Cabins and Holiday Homes**: Renting a cabin or a holiday home is a great way to save money, especially for groups of 6 or more. Many cabins come equipped with kitchens, allowing you to cook your own meals and avoid the high costs of dining out. When booking, look for group-friendly deals, particularly for longer stays. In some rural areas, you can find deals that offer a balance between comfort and affordability.

- **Hotels and Hostels:** Larger groups can save money by booking multiple rooms at a hotel or by choosing hostels that offer group discounts. Many hotels in Norway cater to larger groups and provide discounted rates for bulk bookings. If you're staying in cities like Oslo, Bergen, or Tromsø, check for any special promotions or group packages that may offer reduced rates during the off-season.

- **Group Tours:** Many tour operators in Norway offer special rates for large groups, so consider booking your activities through a tour company. Group bookings often come with discounts for popular attractions, and some tour operators offer all-inclusive packages that include meals, transportation, and guided tours.

4. Transportation Costs for Groups

Getting around Norway can be expensive, especially for larger groups, but there are ways to make transportation more affordable.

- **Bus and Coach Rentals:** Renting a private bus or coach for larger groups (10+ people) is one of the most economical ways to get around. This option is often cheaper than booking individual train tickets or flights for each member of the group. Plus, it allows everyone to stay together, which makes for a more cohesive experience.

- **Trains and Domestic Flights:** For smaller groups or those traveling longer distances, Norway's efficient train system offers group discounts when booked in advance. Alternatively, domestic flights are quick and convenient for reaching distant regions, but they can be costly, so try to book early or look for group airfare deals.

- **Ferries and Cruises:** Many groups traveling to coastal regions can save by booking a group ferry or cruise ticket. Norway's famous fjords and coastal areas are best explored by boat, and group rates on ferries can be a great way to travel in bulk at a reduced cost.

5. Group Activities and Discounted Tours

When planning activities, look for options that offer group discounts. Norway is packed with activities for all types of travelers, from cultural tours to outdoor adventures, and many attractions provide cost savings for group bookings.

- **Outdoor Adventures:** Many outdoor activities, such as hiking or exploring national parks, are free or low-cost, but when booking guided tours (for example, glacier walks or Northern Lights tours), ask about group pricing. Group discounts are commonly offered for larger parties, so don't forget to inquire before making a booking.

- **Cultural and Historical Tours:** If your group is interested in museums, galleries, or historical sites, many of these attractions offer discounted entry for groups. Booking ahead for group tickets to places like the Viking Ship Museum in Oslo or the Bryggen historic district in Bergen can save you money.

- **Adventure and Wildlife Activities:** Norway is known for its adventure sports, including dog sledding, snowshoeing, and whale watching. Many adventure operators offer group rates, so make sure to ask if they have any special offers for larger parties. Whale-watching tours in Tromsø, for instance, can be more affordable per person when booked for a group.

6. Meal Planning and Group Dining

Eating out in Norway can be pricey, so meal planning is a great way to keep your costs in check.

- **Group Meals:** Many restaurants offer set menus or special group deals that can save you money. If you're in a larger group, look for places that cater specifically to groups, as they often offer discounts for bulk orders. Norwegian cuisine is hearty, and a shared meal of fresh fish, meats, or local specialties can be both delicious and affordable when booked as a group.

- **Self-Catering:** If you're staying in a cabin or a holiday home, buying local ingredients and cooking your own meals can significantly lower your food expenses. Norway's grocery stores offer a wide variety of affordable local products, and cooking together can be a fun bonding activity for your group.

- **Street Food:** In cities like Oslo and Bergen, food trucks and casual dining spots offer tasty and affordable options. This can be an excellent choice for lunch or casual dinners, especially for groups on the go.

7. Money-Saving Tips for Group Travel

- **Plan Early and Book Together:** Group discounts are often available for early bookings. Be sure to book transportation, accommodation, and activities well in advance to lock in the best rates.

- **Travel in Off-Peak Seasons:** Avoid the summer months if you want to save money. Fall and spring are ideal times to visit Norway, offering lower prices and fewer crowds.

- **Utilize Local Tourist Passes:** Many cities offer tourist passes that provide discounted or free access to public transport and attractions. Check if there are any available for your destination, as these can save a lot of money for your group.

C. Accessible Travel in Norway

In recent years, this country has made great strides in improving accessibility for all kinds of travelers, from wheelchair users to those with limited mobility. Whether you're exploring urban centers like Oslo or Bergen, or venturing out into the more remote areas, you can rest assured that accessibility is a priority. Let's explore the key points you'll need to know about accessible travel in Norway.

1. Accessible Public Transportation

Norway's public transportation system, including trains, buses, ferries, and trams, has made significant improvements to ensure accessibility for passengers with disabilities.

- **Trains and Rail Services:** Most of Norway's main train stations and trains are accessible to wheelchair users. The national rail operator, Vy, offers dedicated services for travelers with reduced mobility, including accessible carriages, ramps, and assistance with boarding. Some trains also have spaces reserved for wheelchairs, and all trains are equipped with audio and visual announcements for the hearing and visually impaired.

- **Buses and Trams:** In major cities like Oslo and Bergen, buses and trams are fully accessible. These vehicles are equipped with ramps and low floors, making them easy to board for people with wheelchairs or walkers. Many bus stations also have accessible facilities, including elevators and tactile paving for those with visual impairments. For long-distance bus services, be sure to check with the operator in advance to confirm accessibility.

- **Ferries:** Norway's iconic fjords are accessible by boat, and many ferries are equipped with ramps and elevators for easier access. Companies like Fjord1 operate ferries with accessible facilities for travelers with mobility challenges. Some ferries offer free assistance to passengers with disabilities, so it's a good idea to let the staff know when you board.

- **Taxis and Rideshares:** Accessible taxis can be found in most major cities, and these taxis are specially equipped to accommodate passengers with wheelchairs or other mobility aids. Uber and other rideshare services also provide options for accessible vehicles, but be sure to request one in advance to ensure availability.

2. Accessible Accommodation

Norway offers a range of accessible accommodation options, from luxury hotels to charming guesthouses. When booking your stay, it's important to look for properties that meet your specific needs. Many Norwegian hotels and hostels have accessible rooms with wider doors, roll-in showers, and handrails, but it's always a good idea to confirm the details before making a reservation.

- **Hotels and Hostels:** Major hotel chains like Scandic, Radisson Blu, and Thon Hotels offer accessible rooms that include amenities such as accessible bathrooms with roll-in showers, low beds, and visual and auditory signals for alarms. When booking, make sure to mention your accessibility requirements to ensure the room meets your needs.

- **Cottages and Cabins:** If you're staying in rural Norway, look for cabins or holiday homes that are wheelchair-friendly. Many Norwegian cabins are now equipped with accessible entrances, wider doorways, and bathrooms designed for mobility aids. However, always check the specifics before booking.

- **Airbnb and Vacation Rentals:** Airbnb listings in Norway often include accessible homes, but it's important to read the reviews and verify the amenities offered. Many hosts will clearly state whether their property is accessible, and some may offer additional services like helping to arrange transportation or providing specific accessibility features.

3. Accessible Attractions and Sightseeing

From the fjords to the museums, Norway offers a variety of attractions that are accessible to all visitors. Whether you're in Oslo, Bergen, or a remote village, you'll find accessible options for sightseeing and cultural exploration.

- **Museums and Art Galleries:** Many of Norway's top museums, such as the Viking Ship Museum in Oslo and the National Gallery, are accessible to visitors with disabilities. These museums offer ramps, elevators, and wheelchair-friendly facilities. They may also have tactile exhibits for those with visual impairments and audio guides for the hearing impaired.

- **National Parks and Nature:** While Norway's wild landscapes are known for their ruggedness, there are many national parks and nature reserves with accessible paths and viewing areas. For example, the

Hardangervidda National Park has wheelchair-friendly trails, as does Jotunheimen National Park, where you can experience stunning views from accessible lookouts.

- **Norwegian Fjords and Scenic Routes:** Several fjord cruises and sightseeing boat tours are equipped to accommodate travelers with mobility issues. The Nærøyfjord, a UNESCO World Heritage site, offers boat tours with accessible docking areas. In addition, some of Norway's famous scenic routes, like the Atlantic Road, have been designed with accessible viewpoints and rest stops.

- **Historical Sites:** Historical sites such as the Bryggen Hanseatic Wharf in Bergen, and the Kongsberg Silver Mines, offer accessible tours, with routes and facilities designed for those with limited mobility. Some sites also provide assisted tours with guides who are trained to accommodate diverse needs.

4. Accessible Activities and Tours

Norway offers an abundance of activities for visitors with disabilities. Many tour operators and outdoor adventure companies offer tailored experiences that cater to a range of accessibility needs.

- **Northern Lights Tours:** For those wanting to experience the magic of the Northern Lights, there are accessible tours in Tromsø and other northern regions. Many tour companies offer Northern Lights packages with accessible transportation and viewing areas designed for people with mobility challenges.

- **Fjord Cruises:** Several companies offer accessible cruises through the Norwegian fjords, with boats designed to accommodate wheelchairs and other mobility aids. These cruises typically have accessible restrooms and ramps to ensure that everyone can enjoy the majestic landscapes.

- **Dog Sledding and Snowshoeing:** If you're visiting during the winter months, you can still experience outdoor activities like dog sledding and snowshoeing. Some companies in places like Tromsø offer adapted dog sledding tours with modified sleds for wheelchair users. Snowshoeing is also becoming more accessible, with some operators offering snowshoes with wheels to allow for easier mobility on snowy terrains.

- **City Tours:** In cities like Oslo and Bergen, you'll find guided city tours that are specifically designed for those with mobility impairments. These tours are often conducted in accessible vehicles and cover all the major sights, including museums, parks, and historical landmarks.

5. General Travel Tips for Accessible Travel in Norway

- **Plan Ahead:** Norway is an accessible country, but it's always important to plan ahead and ensure that your travel needs are met. Contact hotels, transportation companies, and activity providers in advance to confirm that they can accommodate your specific requirements.

- **Use the Accessibility Assistance:** When booking transportation (whether it's trains, buses, or flights), always let the operator know if you need accessibility assistance. Norwegian rail services, airlines, and bus companies all offer free assistance for people with mobility impairments, but advance notice is essential.

- **Check Local Resources:** Many cities in Norway have local disability organizations that provide helpful resources, including information on accessible transport, tours, and services. Websites like Visit Norway and Disabled Travel offer up-to-date accessibility information for travelers.

- **Stay in Touch:** If you're traveling with a group, make sure to have contact information for the local disability support services, and keep track of your itinerary to ensure you're meeting all your accessibility needs during the trip.

Chapter 11: Must Known Tips

A. Packing List for Norway

I can almost feel your excitement as you plan your adventure to Norway. Trust me, you're in for an unforgettable journey filled with stunning fjords, charming towns, and jaw-dropping landscapes. But before you get swept away by the magic of it all, let's talk about something important—what to pack. Norway's weather is a bit of a trickster, so getting your packing list just right will make all the difference. Let me guide you through it!

Dressing for Norway's Weather

When I first visited Norway, I learned a lesson the hard way—always, always be ready for the weather to change. One minute, it's sunny; the next, you're caught in a rainstorm.

- **Start with a base layer:** Bring thermal tops and leggings, especially if you're visiting in cooler months. They're like your trusty sidekicks, keeping you warm and dry no matter what.
- **Mid-layers are your best friends:** Think fleece jackets or sweaters—something cozy but lightweight. Perfect for layering up or down depending on the day's mood.
- **Outer layers are non-negotiable**: A good waterproof and windproof jacket is essential. Mine saved me more than once when I got caught in sudden rain while hiking Trolltunga.

Oh, and don't forget your pants! Waterproof ones are a game-changer if you're exploring fjords or heading out for an Arctic adventure.

Footwear

Let's talk shoes because your feet deserve the best on this trip.

- **Sturdy hiking boots:** You'll thank yourself when you're trekking up rocky trails or wandering through snow.
- **Comfortable walking shoes:** Exploring cities like Oslo or Bergen means lots of cobblestones and charming streets—your sneakers will be your heroes here.

- **Sandals or light shoes**: Perfect for those summer months when you're cruising the fjords or relaxing by a lake.

I'll share a pro tip: always pack wool socks. They're warm, comfy, and great at keeping your feet dry—Norwegian weather won't stand a chance!

The Little Things That Make a Big Difference

When I was packing for my last trip, I almost forgot these essentials—don't make my mistake!

- **Reusable water bottle:** Norway's tap water is some of the purest in the world. Fill up and save money while staying hydrated.
- **Backpack:** A lightweight, waterproof daypack is perfect for holding your camera, snacks, and those extra layers.
- **Power adapter:** Norway uses Type C and F plugs (230V). Bring a universal adapter to keep your gadgets powered.

And speaking of gadgets, pack a portable charger! Between taking photos, navigating maps, and sharing your journey on social media, your phone battery will thank you.

Toiletries and Health Essentials

Norway's crisp air and adventure-filled days can be tough on your skin. Pack lip balm, sunscreen, and a good moisturizer. Oh, and throw in some bug spray for those summer hikes.

Don't forget a small first-aid kit. A few band-aids and pain relievers can save the day when you're out exploring.

Seasonal Add-Ons

Here's the thing: Norway changes with the seasons, and your packing list should, too.

- **Winter (November–March):** Insulated jackets, gloves, and a hat are your survival kit for the Arctic chill. Hand warmers? Absolute lifesavers!
- **Summer (June–August):** Lighter clothes, quick-dry shorts, and a sunhat will keep you comfy when the sun's shining.
- **Spring and Autumn:** Layers, layers, layers. Think mild weather with a sprinkle of unpredictability.

B. Understanding Norwegian Etiquette and Customs

Understanding local customs and etiquette can help you connect with the people and avoid those "oops" moments. Don't worry—I've got you covered. Let's dive into what makes Norwegians tick and how to blend in like a pro.

The Norwegian Way

First things first, Norwegians value simplicity, modesty, and a strong connection to nature. They're polite but reserved, and you might notice they don't go out of their way to make small talk with strangers. But don't mistake this for coldness—it's just part of their culture. Once you break the ice (pun intended), you'll find Norwegians to be kind, honest, and full of humor.

Greetings:

Forget the hugs and cheek kisses; in Norway, a firm handshake and a friendly "hei" (hi) or "god dag" (good day) will do just fine. Eye contact is important—it shows respect and sincerity. And here's a tip: Norwegians aren't big on formal titles, so feel free to use first names, even in professional settings.

Dining Etiquette:

1. Table Manners:
- Norwegians eat with their fork in their left hand and knife in their right—no switching hands mid-meal.
- Wait for the host to say "vær så god" (please, go ahead) before starting to eat.

2. Sharing the Bill:
- Splitting the bill, or "going Dutch," is common practice. Don't expect someone to pick up the tab unless it's a special occasion.

3. Tipping:
- Tipping isn't mandatory in Norway, but rounding up the bill or leaving 10% is appreciated if the service was exceptional.

Social Etiquette:

Norwegians value their personal space—so don't stand too close in lines, on public transport, or during conversations. They might seem reserved at first, but they're simply respecting your space as much as their own.

Here's a fun fact: Norwegians often leave a seat between themselves and others on buses or trains unless it's crowded. It's not rude—it's just their way of being considerate.

Norway's Famous "Law of Jante"

This unwritten set of social rules emphasizes humility, equality, and not boasting about one's achievements. While it might sound restrictive, it's a cornerstone of Norwegian culture. Bragging or showing off isn't the norm here, so keep it humble and let your experiences speak for themselves.

Respect for Nature: It's in Their DNA

Norwegians are deeply connected to the outdoors, and they take environmental responsibility seriously. Follow their lead by:

- **Leaving No Trace:** Always clean up after yourself, whether you're hiking, picnicking, or camping.
- **Respecting the "Allemannsretten" (Right to Roam):** This law allows everyone to access nature, including private land, as long as you act responsibly.
- **Dressing for the Weather: Locals have a saying:** "There's no such thing as bad weather, only bad clothing." So, pack smart and embrace the outdoors!

Punctuality:

Norwegians value punctuality, whether it's for a dinner party or catching a train. If you're running late, a quick message to inform your host or guide is appreciated. Being on time shows respect for their time—and trust me, they'll notice.

Small Talk and Conversation

Norwegians might not be big on small talk, but they love meaningful conversations. If you want to connect, ask about their favorite hiking spots, winter activities, or local traditions. And don't be surprised if they mention their love for coffee—Norwegians are among the world's top coffee consumers!

Festivals and Celebrations:

If you're lucky enough to visit during a national holiday or festival, join in the celebrations! The most important one is Syttende Mai (May 17th), Norway's Constitution Day. Locals dress in traditional outfits (bunad), wave flags, and parade through the streets. It's a day of pride, joy, and lots of ice cream and hot dogs!

C. Staying Connected

Let's talk about staying connected in Norway—not just to Wi-Fi and mobile networks but also to the people and experiences that make your trip truly memorable.

Mobile Phones and SIM Cards

1. Will Your Phone Work in Norway?
- Most modern smartphones will work in Norway, but check if your device is unlocked and supports European GSM networks.
- Norway uses 4G and 5G networks, so you'll enjoy fast and reliable coverage, even in remote areas.

2. Buying a Norwegian SIM Card
- **Why You Need It:** If you're staying for more than a few days, getting a local SIM card can save you money on roaming fees.
- **Where to Buy:** SIM cards are available at airports, convenience stores like 7-Eleven

and Narvesen, or telecom shops (Telia, Telenor, or Ice).

- **Cost**: Prepaid SIM cards start at around NOK 200 ($20) and include data, calls, and texts.

3. eSIM Option
If your phone supports eSIM, consider purchasing a digital plan before your trip. Providers like Airalo or GigSky offer affordable packages tailored to travelers.

Wi-Fi Access

1. Free Wi-Fi Hotspots
  Where to Find Them:
  - Hotels, cafes, and restaurants almost always offer free Wi-Fi to guests.
  - Many public spaces, including airports, train stations, and libraries, also provide free Wi-Fi.

Pro Tip: If you're in Oslo, look for Oslo Public Wi-Fi—it's free and widely available in the city center.

2. Portable Wi-Fi Devices
  - **Why It's Useful:** A portable Wi-Fi device can be a lifesaver if you're traveling in remote areas where public Wi-Fi is scarce.
  - **Where to Rent:** You can rent devices from companies like Tep Wireless or at major airports.

Apps to Download Before Your Trip

1. Navigation and Transport
   RuterReise: Essential for navigating public transport in Oslo and surrounding areas.
   Vy: Perfect for booking trains and buses across the country.
   Google Maps: A must-have for finding hiking trails, restaurants, and attractions.

2. Language and Communication
   Google Translate: While most Norwegians speak English, this app is handy for signs or menus in Norwegian.
   Duolingo: Learn a few Norwegian phrases before your trip—it's a great way to connect with locals.

3. Staying Informed
   YR.no: Norway's go-to weather app, accurate for planning hikes and outdoor activities.

Staying Connected with Family and Friends

1. International Calls
   If you're using a local SIM card, ensure your plan includes affordable international calls. Alternatively, stick to internet-based options like WhatsApp, Skype, or FaceTime.

2. Social Media Sharing

Norway's landscapes are too beautiful not to share. Use Wi-Fi whenever possible to save data, and make sure your phone's camera is ready for the stunning views!

Emergency Numbers and Communication

1. Emergency Services: Dial 112 for police, 113 for medical emergencies, and 110 for fire services.
2. Tourist Help Lines: Visit Norway's official site offers contact options for assistance.

Tips for Staying Connected in Remote Areas

Norway's remote fjords and mountain regions are beautiful but can have limited network coverage.

- **Offline Maps:** Download maps and transport schedules in advance. Google Maps and Maps.me both offer offline functionality.
- **Backup Power**: Bring a portable charger to keep your devices powered during long days exploring.
- **Check Coverage:** Providers like Telenor and Telia have extensive networks, but remote areas might still have dead zones.

CONCLUSION

We've now reached the end of this comprehensive yet accessible guide to Norway for 2025. It's been a true pleasure to share with you the many wonders of this remarkable country. From the stunning landscapes to the rich culture and vibrant culinary scene, I hope this guide has equipped you with the knowledge and inspiration to craft a truly unforgettable Norwegian adventure.

As you know, travel conditions can shift quickly, so I encourage you to stay informed and up to date with any changes that might impact your plans. Make sure to check travel websites, local news, and community updates to ensure you have all the information you need for a smooth and enjoyable journey. Social media platforms, travel blogs, and local forums can offer real-time tips, insider advice, and personal stories that will make your experience even more enriching.

Thank you for choosing this guide to accompany you on your journey. I truly hope you have an incredible time exploring the awe-inspiring beauty, culture, and history of Norway in 2025. Safe travels, and who knows, maybe our paths will cross someday on the scenic roads or in the charming villages of this magnificent country!

Made in the USA
Monee, IL
13 January 2025